The World's
GREATEST
SPIES
and
SPYMASTERS

The World's
GREATEST
SPIES
and
SPYMASTERS

Roger Boar
&
Nigel Blundell

OCTOPUS BOOKS

Acknowledgements

The publishers wish to thank the following organizations for their kind permission to reproduce the pictures in this book:
Mary Evans Picture Library 11, 19; Thames Television Ltd 2 below left and 22; All other pictures supplied by Topham Picture Library.

The authors wish to thank Jitka Markova, for patience and encouragement, and Robin Corry, Robert Gibson and Tony Harris for research and contributions. They also wish to apologize to Natalie for not sharing as much of her first two months of life as they might have done.

First published in 1984
by Octopus Books Limited
59 Grosvenor Street
London W1

© 1984 Octopus Books Limited

ISBN 0 7064 2032 2

Second impression, reprinted 1984
Reprinted 1985

Made and printed in Great Britain by
Richard Clay (The Chaucer Press) Limited
Bungay, Suffolk

Contents

Chapter
One

Past Masters

Today spying is a full-time, worldwide occupation involving millions of agents, billions of pounds, and the latest ultra-sophisticated technology. But it was not always that way . . .

Spying: the Necessary Evil

Espionage agents have existed since man first learned to wage war. 'Those who know the enemy as well as they know themselves will never suffer defeat,' wrote Chinese military expert Sun Tzu in the 4th century BC. Foreknowledge, he added, enables sovereigns and commanders 'to strike and conquer and achieve things beyond the reach of ordinary men'. Over the centuries all the great generals have proved his words true.

Hannibal's successful Carthaginian invasion of Italy via the Alps in 218 BC owed less to the elephants immortalized by history books than to years spent cultivating a network of informers among Gaulish tribes in the Po valley. They told him about his enemy's strengths, the sympathies of the people ruled by Rome, the layout of the land, how the climate affected it and where to find food and fresh water.

When Genghis Khan's Mongol hordes invaded Europe in the 13th century, their way was prepared by locally recruited spies posing as merchants and traders. A pony post, with fresh couriers and horses waiting to take over at 25-mile staging posts, enabled information to reach the Khan in 24 hours instead of the 10 days taken for normal travel. This was the inspiration behind the Pony Express in America's Wild West many centuries later.

One of the reasons Oliver Cromwell was able to dethrone King Charles I in the British Civil War of the 1640s was that, unlike the Royalists, he valued intelligence. His chief scout was Sir Samuel Luke. It was said he was so industrious in snooping on the enemy that 'they eat, sleep, drink not, whisper not, but he can give us an account of their darkest proceedings'.

Forty years later, John Churchill, first Duke of Marlborough, told critics of his enormous expenditure on espionage: 'No war can be conducted successfully without early and good intelligence, and such advices cannot be had but at very great expense.' Marlborough never forgot the fiasco of the Battle of Sedgemoor in 1685, when a spy gave the rebel Duke of Monmouth full details of the arms and strength of the Royal army camped nearby, but forgot to mention a water-filled ditch. When Monmouth's infantry launched a surprise night raid, the chaos caused by the ditch gave the Royalists time to wake and rout the rebels. Monmouth was beheaded nine days later.

But the generals history remembers were the exception rather than the rule. Although there were always people ready to provide information at a price, too often their customers disregarded it, preferring to rely on their own preconceived ideas. For centuries sovereigns and commanders echoed the words of Lord Raglan in the official British history of the disastrous Crimean War: 'The gathering of knowledge by clandestine means is repulsive to the feelings of gentlemen.'

Spying ceased to be a despised private enterprise in Britain only when the realm was in peril. Queen Elizabeth I was fortunate that her subjects included the man widely regarded as the first great spymaster, Sir Francis Walsingham. He bankrupted himself protecting the Protestant Queen Elizabeth I from Catholic plots and the threat from Spain. Sir Francis Drake took the popular credit for defeating the Armada in 1588, but it was Walsingham and his spies who made it possible.

Walsingham was a rarity in early espionage, a man who used information for national, not personal, ends. When the Queen proved mean about providing him with funds, he paid his network from his own pocket, declaring: 'Knowledge is never too dear.' He was also ruthless in the cause. When playwright Christopher Marlowe, who had been recruited at Cambridge University to infiltrate a Jesuit ring of plotters in Rheims, was discovered making plots of his own against the crown, Walsingham sent three men to murder him at a Deptford tavern.

Most nations relied on ambassadors at foreign courts for intelligence. Walsingham placed his faith in patriotic young students fresh out of college. He was convinced his Queen would never be safe while her younger relative, Mary, lived as a figurehead for Catholic insurrection. Gilbert Gifford, a young Catholic who offered his services to Walsingham while in jail for fraud, was placed on her staff. He read her secret messages, concealed in beer barrels and wine bottles, and also obtained the Papal code, which enabled Walsingham to read all intercepted correspondence from the Vatican. This unmasked the Anthony Babington plot to topple Elizabeth and replace her on the throne with Mary. Walsingham could put Mary on trial, and ensure her execution.

The Spanish threat proved more difficult to deal with, but again Walsingham's resourceful agents were at hand. Richard Gibbes, posing as a Scottish supporter of Mary, travelled through Spain and reported at least 150 galleons in different ports being prepared for an invasion. Anthony Standen, working from Florence, persuaded the newly-appointed Tuscan ambassador to Madrid, Giovanni Figliazzi, to provide information. He discovered a man whose brother was a servant to the Marquis of Santa Cruz, Grand Admiral of the Spanish Navy, and through him, obtained copies of a report to King Philip detailing the number of ships available for the Armada, their guns, stores, and even outlining how many sailors, soldiers and slaves there were aboard each. He also warned that the fleet planned to sail in 1587.

Walsingham acted fast. In April Sir Francis Drake sent fire ships into Cadiz harbour in the famous raid to 'singe the King of Spain's beard'. When Philip tried to arrange loans with Genoese merchants to repair the damage, Walsingham had already put pressure on the money-lenders to delay the Armada further. Then, with the help of astrologer John Dee, he launched a disinformation campaign throughout Europe. Independent star-gazers prophesied unusually bad weather during 1588. Dee embroidered upon the gloomy prediction, telling envoys who were sure to report back to Spain, that violent storms and the destruction of a great empire were certain at around the time the Armada was due to sail. Morale in Madrid slumped. When sailing day dawned, Walsingham's agents charted the Spanish fleet's course all the way. Their activities had given England time to prepare for the invasion attempt. When the galleons at last reached Britain, the promised storms helped Drake and the outnumbered Elizabethan fleet to inflict a defeat so crushing that Spain was no longer a danger. Walsingham, the man who masterminded the victory, died in poverty in 1590. A Spanish agent wrote from London to King Philip: 'There is much sorrow.' The King noted cryptically: 'There, yes. But it is good news here!'

It was more than a century before Britain again established an efficient espionage system. With the country in no immediate peril, Elizabeth's successor, James I, dubbed 'the wisest fool in Christendom', dissipated his intelligence forces by indulging in bizarre hunts for alleged witches. The Stuarts paid dearly for neglecting to keep informed and Cromwell, who took advantage of that fact in 1645, was determined not to make the same mistake. John Thurloe, a mild, modest Essex lawyer, was installed security chief with an annual budget of £70,000 – 20 times more than was available to Walsingham. In return he built up a spy network at home and abroad that earned this grudging praise from the Venetian ambassador Sagredo: 'There is no government on earth which divulges its affairs less than England, or is more punctually informed of those in others.'

Thurloe infiltrated spies into Royalist camps abroad, spending generously because good agents 'cannot be gained but by money; for money they will do anything'. Although exiled King Charles II offered a knighthood and £5,000 to the person who assassinated Cromwell, the Protector died in his bed because Thurloe knew of every Royalist plot in advance.

Thurloe also had agents in every court in Europe. He knew within days what happened when the French Cabinet met behind locked doors; Jewish refugees fleeing from persecution in Europe put their well-established chains of correspondents at his disposal. Ambassador Sagredo noted that Jesuit priests were bribed in Rome, and 'in France, Spain, Germany and at Venice they have insignificant persons who from time to time send important advices,

Charles II paid no heed to intelligence gathering after his restoration to the throne in 1660. He suffered the Stuart delusions about the divine right of kings, despite the beheading of his father 11 years earlier. But his cousin, Louis XIV of France, was made of sterner stuff. Anxious to know what England was up to during negotiations for the Treaty of Dover, he sent Louise de la Quérouaille to London as a spy. Her beauty quickly caught the lusty King's eye, and she was soon a regular mistress. She became Duchess of Portsmouth, and was said to have conceived one of his children between horse races at Newbury.

and being less under observation, penetrate everywhere'.

At home, Thurloe took control of the country by dividing it up into 11 districts, each commanded by an army major general, and policed by a militia. Correspondence was shamelessly intercepted and read, and informing on neighbours was encouraged by financial reward. Such 'protective custody' was abused as the puritan Parliamentarians closed down inns and carried on vendettas against suspected Royalists, but as an espionage exercise, its success was unparalleled in British history. Unfortunately for Thurloe, Cromwell's death in 1658 was the beginning of his own end. Many Parliamentarians pledged secret support to the King whose restoration became much more likely.

With the return of the Stuarts in 1660, organized espionage on a national and international scale was virtually non-existent in Britain until the 1914-18 war. But other nations followed where Walsingham and Thurloe led ...

Steiber: the Sinister Trendsetter

European countries, with their long land frontiers and greater vulnerability to unexpected invasions, appreciated the need for spies more than island Britain. France, Russia and Germany have always invested heavily in espionage, and each has produced great spies and spymasters. Napoleon Bonaparte had replaced Louis as France's ruler. The Corsican-born dictator had no love for espionage, saying once that 'a spy is a natural traitor'. But he realized the value of secret agents in defending his regime, and used one to great effect. Karl Schulmeister arrived in Vienna pretending to be a nobleman kicked out of Paris as an Austrian spy. Within months the schemer described as 'a man all brains and no heart' had been appointed Austrian head of military intelligence. Cunningly recruiting two Austrian officers to confirm his reports to army commander Marshal Mack von Leiberich, he completely undermined the country's defences. Napoleon's armies gained devastating victories in the battles of Ulm and Austerlitz because Schulmeister had given them the entire Austrian battle orders.

When Napoleon declared another war in 1803, the startled British were taken completely by surprise. Invasion plans were halted by Nelson's victories at sea, notably in the Battle of Trafalgar. And in July 1808, Britain at last got the chance to strike back on land. Spain asked London for help when Napoleon imposed his brother Joseph on the throne of Madrid. Whitehall sent an army commanded by probably the greatest military spymaster of all time.

Sir Arthur Wellesley, later Duke of Wellington, who defeated Napoleon at Waterloo in 1815, was probably the greatest military spymaster of all time. He lived by the motto: 'All the business of war is to find out what you don't know by what you do.' He always studied the enemy in depth, finding out not only where the opposing army was and how strong it was, but the character of its commanders, the spirit and training of its troops, their battle experience, and how they were supplied with arms and rations. He sent expert horsemen out to map the roads, rivers and topography of the theatre of war; if thunderstorms could turn a dry river bed into a torrent, he wanted to know. His outriders also assessed the local population for their attitude to the British.

Efficient espionage helped Napoleon rule France and his conquered territory until Wellington's military might toppled him on the muddy slopes of Mont St Jean, Waterloo.

With France crushed, and Britain intent on building a far-flung empire, the way was clear for Germany to achieve its dream of Teutonic mastery of Europe. Otto von Bismarck was the ruler who united the Germanic states under powerful Prussia, but Wilhelm Johann Karl Eduard Steiber, born in Merseburg in 1818, was the man who made it possible. His thorough organization and ruthlessness, his sinister innovations and cold, calculating manipulation of human weakness made him the spymaster who most shaped the course of 20th-century espionage.

Steiber started his life of subterfuge as a lawyer in Berlin. He built a reputation as a friend and defender of radicals. In fact, he betrayed them to the police once he won their confidence. He even turned in his wife's uncle. His double-dealing earned him the post of police commissioner in 1850, but when his patron, King Frederick William, was declared insane five years later, Steiber fell from grace as Prussians sickened by his upstart lack of principles and gentlemanly breeding took revenge.

Steiber wisely fled abroad. While commissioner he had covered up a scandal involving a Russian diplomat, so he went to St Petersburg to test the Tsar's gratitude. The Russian royal family relied heavily on their secret police for protection, and Steiber was asked to reorganize the dreaded Ochrana. He tightened its grip on the Russian people, and extended its tentacles outside the country, sending agents to terrorize dissidents who had sought sanctuary throughout Europe. Once Steiber visited London, where he checked on Prussian refugees such as Karl Marx. For while apparently serving the Tsar, he was sending intelligence to Prussia, trying to re-establish himself in his homeland.

The ploy worked. In 1863 he was introduced to Bismarck as a 'useful man' and taken back into Prussian service. Austria was to be the next addition to the German empire, and Steiber was sent to check its military preparedness. He travelled the country as a pedlar with two boxes on his cart. One contained religious statuettes, the other pornographic pictures. If customers spurned one of his special offers, they usually went for the other. Months later he returned to Bismarck with a complete, accurate picture of Austria's strengths. He reported that its army was still using out-of-date muzzle-loading rifles, no match for the Germans' breech-loading guns. General Helmuth von Moltke knew he could attack with confidence. After a seven-week war, the Austrians surrendered after the horrific battle of Sadowa on 3 July 1866 had left 40,000 of their men dead. Prussia lost only 9,000.

Steiber, now described by Bismarck as 'my king of sleuthhounds', then instituted the most ruthless counter-espionage system the world had seen. There was strict, regular censorship of letters and telegrams, and anyone even suspected of spying on Prussia was summarily shot. He set up the Green House, a Berlin centre for every vice and perversion, to blackmail people of consequence. And he deliberately created a climate of fear and suspicion.

By 1868 it was clear to Bismarck that French opposition was the only obstacle to uniting Germany. Steiber and two accomplices moved into France, and for 18 months lived there undetected, learning every military, political and economic fact that might be remotely useful to an invading army. Armament factories, local geography, the attitude of the population to their government, their grievances about taxes, were as important to him as the latest reports on the new French machine gun, and the preparedness of the nation's armed forces. He returned to Berlin with three trunks full of the most detailed dossier ever assembled on a potential enemy. On 19 July 1870, Prussia invaded. Just over six weeks later, France surrendered. Steiber then launched a murderous secret war on any dissidents, even executing residents who happened to look out of their windows as Prussian troops marched by.

When the king of sleuthhounds died in 1892, it was said aristocrats throughout Europe flocked to his funeral not to mourn, but to make sure he was really dead. Later secret services, notably those of the Nazis and the Soviet Union, were to adopt his ruthless methods, and even develop new forms of inhumanity. But distaste for organized espionage still persisted among Europe's ruling classes. For most nations, spying was the Great Game portrayed by Rudyard Kipling in his Kim stories. Britain, despite the shocks caused by lack of intelligence in the Crimea, the Indian Mutiny and the Boer Wars of South Africa, continued to rely on eccentric amateurs for information. Bismarck's success in France caused Whitehall chiefs to dust the cobwebs off their disused military intelligence HQ in Horse Guards Parade. They found unopened dispatches from abroad that were 20 years old.

Military leaders relied on the services of young adventurers who enjoyed the 'sport' of fortress hunting. Even Germany had rebelled against the Steiber savagery of killing convicted spies, and a British Grenadier guard was able to recommend espionage in Europe as great fun, adding: 'The risk of fines and imprisonment gives a delicious zest to it.' Robert Baden-Powell, later to found the Boy Scout movement, was one of the roving patriots who toured potential enemy strongholds posing as a botanist or landscape painter, incorporating the lines of defences in sketches of butterfly wings or picturesque ports. Dashes and dots in the drawings denoted the number and calibre of guns.

Finally Whitehall realized that, with storm clouds gathering over Europe, such hit-and-miss espionage was not enough. On 23 August 1909, a new military intelligence organization was set up. MO5 consisted of Captain Vernon Kell, of the South Staffordshire Regiment. He was given a small office in the War Office, one assistant, and told to keep his spending to a minimum. Five years later, Kell pulled off one of the greatest coups of World War 1 ...

Vernon Kell: Curse of the Kaiser

German agents began infiltrating Britain to prepare for World War 1 as early as 1902. The authorities took little interest. Then, with the setting up of MO5, later renamed MI5, the police at last found someone who took their espionage warnings seriously. And Vernon Kell, taking on the might of German intelligence single-handed, realized Scotland Yard's Special Branch men were vital allies. He started close co-operation with Superintendent Patrick Quinn. It paid off just 12 months later.

Kaiser Wilhelm II came to London in 1910 for the funeral of King Edward VII. In his party was a naval captain known to be a spymaster. He was trailed to a seedy barber's shop run by Karl Gustav Ernst in the Caledonian

The Kaiser

Road. It was an unlikely choice for a gentleman who only wanted a haircut. Kell applied for permission to intercept the barber's mail. He discovered that Ernst was Germany's intelligence post-master. Berlin sent him packages containing individual letters of instructions for their agents, to be posted in London. The agents sent back their reports via Ernst's shop.

Kell and Quinn now played a waiting game. Detectives kept watch on every agent unmasked, but it was vital not to alert them to this fact because the Germans would then replace them, or find new ways of contacting them. It was also important to trace every member of each agent's network. Only when it became obvious that crucial secrets were about to be relayed to Berlin did the counter-espionage forces strike. Where possible, information and instructions were merely doctored by the interceptors, sometimes using expert forgers from Parkhurst jail. But some arrests were essential – if there were none the Germans might smell a rat.

One of Kell's problems was that espionage was not taken seriously by the law. German army lieutenant Siegfried Helm, caught red-handed making detailed sketches of Portsmouth's dockyard defences, was merely bound over to keep the peace and released by a court. Spying in peacetime was not considered an offence.

Kell campaigned for changes in the Official Secrets Act, and in 1911 it was amended to cover collection of information which might be useful to an enemy in future wars. Kell could now prosecute such spies as Dr Armgaard Karl Graves, jailed for 18 months at Edinburgh for snooping on the Navy's Rosyth base and collecting information about weapons from Glasgow companies; Heinrich Grosse, tried at Winchester in 1912 after amassing a huge dossier on ships, submarines and artillery at Portsmouth; and Frederick Adolphus Schroeder, imprisoned for six years in April 1914. As Frederick Gould, he used German intelligence funds to buy the Queen Charlotte public house in Rochester, near the top-secret Chatham dockyard, in 1902. Kell had known about him since 1911, but only pounced when his wife set out by train for Brussels with sensitive data on guns, cruisers and minefields in her bag.

Kell's finest hour came when war was declared on 4 August 1914. Before dawn on the following day, he and the Special Branch, now led by Sir Basil Thomson, had arrested Ernst the barber – paid £1 a month by the Germans – and 23 other spies. Germany's entire intelligence network in Britain was wiped out as agents were seized in London, Newcastle, Barrow in Furness, Portsmouth, Southampton, Brighton, Falmouth and Warwick. German armies battling the French near Mons were amazed to encounter British troops when they tried to outflank their enemy. The British Expeditionary Force had slipped unnoticed across the Channel to the trenches. The furious Kaiser exclaimed: 'Am I surrounded by dolts? Why have I never been told we have no spies in England.' Gustav Steinhauer, who called himself the Kaiser's Master Spy, had no answer.

The Germans tried to form a new network, but with little success. Kell and Thomson supplemented their vigilance with newspaper propaganda campaigns whipping up spy hysteria, and reports of suspect neighbours flooded in. One spy, posing as a Norwegian journalist, was suspected because he was too quiet in his rooms. Detectives discovered invisible ink in a bottle marked gargling lotion.

Two Dutchmen arrived in Portsmouth, posing as cigar salesmen. Their reports to Rotterdam were disguised as orders, 5,000 Coronas representing five warships about to sail. Kell's postal censors were puzzled by the sudden popularity of cigars in Hampshire and detectives were called in. The two spies were arrested and shot. Another agent toured Britain as a music hall trick-cyclist. Censors discovered messages in invisible ink on English songsheets he was sending to Zurich.

Kell made brilliant use of another detected spy. Carl Hans Lody, a German naval reserve officer who had been living in America, landed in Scotland posing as an American tourist in September 1914. He immediately sent a telegram to his contact in Sweden saying, 'Hope we beat these damned Germans soon.' It was a suspicious communication between representatives of countries supposed to be neutral. Lody was tailed as he travelled round England. The watchdogs could not believe their luck when they discovered he was sending to Germany as fact a British propaganda story stating that Russian troops were landing in Scotland to reinforce the Allies in the European trenches. Lody was later nicknamed the spy who cost Germany the war. Two divisions were withdrawn to watch Channel ports for the Russian arrival, weakening the Kaiser's forces for the vital Battle of the Marne which the Germans might otherwise have won. Lody was eventually arrested and shot at the Tower of London in November 1916.

British intelligence also detected the amorous activities of over-rated sex spy Mata Hari. Gertrud Margarete Zelle, born in Holland, took the name Mata Hari (it meant Eye of the Morning) when she became an erotic dancer in Paris. During the war, she cashed in on the pleasure sex gave her by sleeping with important military figures on both sides, and selling what they told her to the enemy. In Paris, Berlin and Madrid, she plied her erotic espionage trade, though the secrets she passed were seldom of much value. In 1916, her ship to Holland docked at Falmouth, and she was escorted to London for interrogation. If she persisted in consorting with the Germans, she was warned, she would be in trouble. Mata took no notice. She was later arrested by the French, and shot on 15 October 1917.

Only one spy escaped the notice of Kell and Thomson – they only learned about him when he wrote his memoirs back in Germany in 1925. Jules Silber could pass as an Englishman after travels in India, America and South Africa. He fought for the British in the Boer Wars, which helped gain him a job in the postal censor's office when he turned up in London in 1914, offering his services. He regularly sent the Kaiser dossiers on what he learned from reading other people's letters. His own mail went undetected because he could stamp it 'passed by the censor'. Silber's most spectacular success was warning Germany about the Q-ships. A girl wrote that her brother was involved in a strange scheme to put guns on old merchant ships. Silber posed as a censor to call on her and warn against future indiscretions. Before he left,

Mata Hari

she had revealed all he needed to know about the innocent-looking cargo carriers camouflaged to protect Atlantic convoys against German submarine attack.

Silber's information was a rare naval coup for the Kaiser's fleet. For most of the war, British Naval Intelligence under Admiral Sir Reginald Hall – nicknamed Blinker because of a nervous tic in one eye – ruled both the ocean and air waves. Hours after hostilities began, a British ship sliced a hundred yards of cable out of Germany's main under-water telecommunications link with the outside world. This forced the Kaiser's forces to send messages by radio, which could be intercepted at listening stations along the English south coast. The messages were then decyphered in Room 40 of the Admiralty building in London, using naval code books taken during an engagement with the German cruiser *Magdeburg* on 26 August.

Hall got his hands on the enemy's diplomatic code when a German guerrilla harrying British forces in Turkey fled abandoning his baggage. When a new German transmitter began broadcasts from Brussels, using another code, Naval Intelligence learned that the staff included a British-born cypher clerk called Alexander Szek, who still had relatives living near Croydon in London. Szek agreed to copy the code book, piece by piece. When he completed the task, he vanished. Mystery still surrounds exactly what happened. The British said the Germans discovered his treachery and executed him. French sources claimed a British agent smuggled Szek out of Brussels to prevent the Germans learning their code was broken, then pushed him off ship in the middle of the English Channel to ensure he stayed silent. Another version is that he died in a hit-and-run 'accident' in a Brussels side street. Whatever the cause, Szek's death proved that the British no longer considered espionage a game. It was now a matter of life and death.

Control of the German codes enabled Admiral Sir Reginald Hall to fool the Kaiser with deliberately false messages. In September 1916 he arranged for one of his agents to leak an emergency code to the Germans, then signalled that ships were sailing from Dover, Harwich and Tilbury with troops to invade the north Belgian coast. To authenticate the information, he had 25 special editions of the *Daily Mail* newspaper printed, with a spurious story about preparations at 'an East Coast base'. Copies were smuggled to Holland, and passed surreptitiously to German agents. The ploy worked almost too well. The German High Command detached a large force from the trenches and moved it to the coast. But a War Office agent, not told of the subterfuge, warned Whitehall the movement heralded a plan to invade England. The War Office started preparing to evacuate south-east England until it was let in on Hall's secret.

Hall's most significant part in winning the war was the Zimmermann Telegram. The code Szek provided enabled Room 40 decipherers to read a message from the German Secretary of State, Arthur Zimmermann, to his ambassador in Mexico City in January 1917, warning that unrestricted submarine attacks on neutral Atlantic convoys were about to start, and instructing the envoy to organise Mexican attacks on the southern United States if America entered the war. Hall ensured that the message reached the White House in a way which clearly proved it was not a British invention. Together with the sinking of the liner *Lusitania*, the telegram forced the United States to abandon its policy of isolation three months later. It was the turning point in Allied fortunes.

Hall, Thomson and Kell had done as much as anyone to earn the victory that finally came on 11 November, 1918. They were abetted by Commander Mansfield Cumming, first chief of the Special Intelligence Section, later MI6, which was founded in 1912 for offensive espionage abroad. One of his agents is said to have alerted Hall's Naval Intelligence to the possibility of using Alexander Szek to obtain the Kaiser's code. His name was Sidney Reilly ...

Reckless Reilly: Ace of Spies

The history of espionage has produced no greater enigma than Sidney Reilly. Both his birth and death are shrouded in mystery. But his achievements were unquestionable. Beyond doubt he was a ruthless agent and a relentless womanizer whose exploits put even the fictional adventures of 007 James Bond in the shade. Bond's creator Ian Fleming said: '007 was just a piece of nonsense I dreamed up. He was not a Sidney Reilly, you know.'

Though he later carried passports giving his birthplace as Tipperary, Ireland, Reilly was probably born in southern Russia, near Odessa, on 24 March 1874. At 19 he is said to have discovered that the Russian army colonel married to his mother was not his father. He had been conceived during her affair with a Viennese doctor, and his real name was Sigmund Georgievich Rosenblum. The shock of finding he was Jewish, made the youngster flee anti-semitic Russia. He stowed away on a British boat to South America, and worked as a docker, road-mender and plantation hand. Then, according to his own story, he was recruited as cook for a British expedition into the wilds of the Amazon. When natives attacked the camp, Reilly's sharpshooting scared them off.

Impressed by his courage, and his fluency in several languages, including Russian and German, the leader of the party, Major Fothergill, gave him £1,500 and offered him a secret service post. Reilly began work as a freelance.

He took the name Reilly from his first wife. Margaret Reilly Thomas was 23, lively and attractive when the spy met her in Europe. She was touring with her dour, bad-tempered husband Hugh, a Non-Conformist minister

Sidney Reilly

from Wales. He was wealthy, 60 years old, and, Margaret told Reilly, a sadist who beat her viciously. Reilly started staying in hotel rooms just across the corridor from theirs. Margaret slipped into his bed surreptitiously as her husband slept under the influence of increasingly large doses of laudanum from Reilly, who was posing as a medical expert. When the Reverend Thomas fell seriously ill at his London home, Reilly suggested a Continental trip to get him away from prying neighbours. At Newhaven, en route to the Europe ferry, Thomas died. Margaret inherited £8,000. Five months later she became the first Mrs Reilly. She was not the last. And Thomas was not the last man Reilly murdered.

The new century found him in Holland, posing as a German, checking Dutch aid to the Boers in South Africa. Reilly had an uncanny knack of being able to see the world's trouble-spots and getting in early. He realized the potential of the oil discoveries in the Middle East. Britain, he warned, was in danger of missing out. He went to Persia and discovered the Shah had granted development rights to an Australian, William D'Arcy, who was in Cannes discussing financial backing with the wealthy Rothschilds. Reilly disguised himself as a priest and walked brazenly on to the family yacht in the French harbour, touting for charity cheques. While the hosts wrote them out, he drew D'Arcy to one side and promised that the British government would top any offer the Rothschilds made. In May 1905, D'Arcy was given £900,000 of shares in the company formed to cash in on the opportunity Reilly provided – British Petroleum, better known today as BP.

Reilly spent the next few years in the Far East gathering details of Russia's naval strength and eastern defences.

But by 1914 he was back in Europe, embarking on a series of missions which almost defied belief, and earned him the British Military Cross. Before war broke out in 1914, he secured a job at the giant Krupp armaments factory in Essen under the alias Karl Hahn. He volunteered for extra night shifts, and broke into the top-secret drawing offices to scrutinize every detail of the weapons' production schedule. When he was discovered, he killed two watchmen to escape.

Back in Russia, he posed as a wealthy businessman and organised the St Petersburg flying week. German visitors eagerly confided secrets of aircraft development. The extraordinary spy then persuaded German naval builders Blohm and Voss to make him their sole agent for exports to Russia. He earned huge commissions as a salesman, and was so successful that Britons in St Petersburg complained to their ambassador that he was robbing British companies of orders. Reilly became rich, and London received blueprints and specifications of the Kaiser's most up-to-date warships.

The British secret service was getting so much priceless information from

Reilly that it had to accept him on his own terms. Spy chiefs knew, or suspected, he was selling the intelligence he sent them to other powers, particularly Russia and later France. And they were powerless to prevent him taking the audacious risks which earned him the nickname Reckless Reilly. They even had to turn a blind eye to his bigamous marriage when Margaret refused a cash offer to agree to a divorce. Reilly forced her to leave St Petersburg, then married Countess Massino, ex-wife of a Russian government minister.

By 1917, Reilly was back in London. Though over 40, he volunteered to pioneer a new kind of espionage parachuting behind enemy lines to collect information. He was dropped near Mannheim, with forged papers claiming he had been invalided out of the German army, and in three weeks picked up vital data about the offensive planned by the Germans for 1918. The attack, which might have won the war, was countered. Reilly later posed as a German officer, and spent several days in a mess at Konigsberg, East Prussia, collecting the latest war gossip. And his greatest triumph was to sit in at a High Command conference attended by the Kaiser himself.

Reilly had somehow established himself as driver to an officer on the staff of Prince Rupprecht of Bavaria. As they drove to the war council, the British spy pretended there was an engine fault, and lifted the car bonnet to investigate. When the impatient officer joined him in the dark of the lonely forest road, Reilly quietly killed him with a blow to the head, donned his uniform, and drove on to the meeting, coolly making apologies for his late arrival by saying his driver had been taken ill. He then sat taking notes of all future battle plans, and was able to warn the British Admiralty of a submarine offensive to cripple Atlantic supply lines. U-boat commanders found their targets protected by heavily armed convoys.

In April 1918, Reilly was sent back to Russia. The Bolsheviks had seized power the previous year, and seemed likely to make peace with the Germans, freeing the entire might of the Kaiser for an offensive on the Western Front. British Prime Minister David Lloyd George sanctioned an attempted overthrow of the communists to prevent the pact, and Reilly was the only man who might just bring it about. Using a pass provided by a contact in the new Soviet secret police, the Cheka, Reilly set about organizing cells of resistance. He raised more than two million roubles from White Russian sympathizers, and also used £120,000 of the British government's money to bribe influential figures.

The bizarre plan was to kidnap Soviet leaders Lenin and Trotsky and parade them through the streets in their underpants, objects of ridicule. Reilly even selected an alternative government, with himself as prime minister. But the congress at which the leaders were to be seized was unexpectedly postponed. Then another anti-Bolshevik, Dora Kaplan, tried to kill Lenin. He survived, though hit twice by her bullets, and a savage purge by the Cheka was launched. Most of Reilly's accomplices were rounded up.

Reilly was at the British consulate at St Petersburg when the Cheka called. A courageous naval captain called Cromie died holding them at bay with two pistols long enough for Reilly to flee through a window. Though the Bolsheviks put a price of 100,000 roubles on his head, Reilly survived for two months, posing as a Russian peasant, a Greek traveller and a Turkish merchant before reaching safety aboard a Dutch trading ship.

Back in London, Reilly divorced Nadine and married actress Pepita Bobadilla, again bigamously. He remained obsessed with the need to overthrow the Russian regime, and began working with Boris Savinkoff, once a revolutionary but now one of Lenin's fiercest foes in exile. Both men were intrigued at the emergence of The Trust, said to be an organization of influential Russians committed to overthrowing Lenin and restoring democracy. Savinkoff went to Moscow to find out more about the rebels. A year later, in 1925, Reilly followed. He was never seen in the West again.

At first it was thought he was shot trying to cross the Finnish border into Russia. His new wife inserted a death notice in newspapers, saying Soviet troops killed him near Allekul on 28 September. But she believed he was still alive. The notice was an attempt to force a statement from either the British or Russian authorities. Both stayed tight-lipped. Over the next five years, refugees from Soviet oppression spoke of seeing Reilly inside Butyrski prison hospital. Some said he was insane after torture. Then more sinister leaks began emerging. A Finn claimed the master spy knew The Trust was a Soviet scheme to entice enemies of the state into the Cheka's grip, but was hoping to 're-organize Bolshevism if he could not defeat it'.

During World War 2, Soviet defector Walter Krivitsky alleged information from Reilly helped Russia penetrate the British secret service and Foreign Office. 'He thought by telling us a little he could help Britain and save himself.' said Krivitsky. 'In the end he did not help Britain and he did not save himself.' In 1966 a Russian magazine said Reilly, when arrested, offered to tell all he knew about British and American intelligence networks. And in 1972, a Paris newspaper claimed Reilly was a Soviet agent all along.

Only the KGB's files are likely to ever unlock the last riddle surrounding Reilly. A television series on his life, shown in Britain in 1983, described him as the ace of spies. No agent has ever achieved so much so audaciously, even though security in every state was far less efficient than it is today. He was a legend in his own lifetime – and may have left a devastating legacy. If, as Krivitsky and others claimed, he told the Russians, either voluntarily or under torture, how to infiltrate the British Establishment, Sidney Reilly laid the foundations for a spy ring whose exploits almost matched his own ...

Chapter Two

Cambridge Circus Spies

The carnage of World War 1 and the terror of Russia's Bolshevik Revolution had turned Rudyard Kipling's Great Game into a serious business. It was about to become even more sinister. And, ironically, one of the men who made it so took his name from Kipling's hero, Kim . . .

Moscow Mole Philby Burrows Deep

Cambridge University was for decades a bastion of privilege, a stepping stone for the moneyed elite progressing from public school to public office. In a rarified atmosphere, snugly shielded from the harsh realities of life, bright young things whiled away three years study with the self-assured arrogance of a class whose right to rule the country had never been questioned. But in the 1930s a new breed with a new creed began to graduate from the cloistered quadrangles. They were the Communist super spies – Guy Burgess, Donald Maclean, Kim Philby, Anthony Blunt and a fifth man who, according to espionage experts, is only protected from the disgrace he deserves by the libel laws.

The damage the infamous five inflicted on Britain, America and totally innocent third parties has still not been fully assessed, 50 years after they espoused the Soviet cause. One British Foreign Office spokesman said: 'Philby robbed European countries of their freedom.' A CIA man told journalists: 'From 1944 to 1951, the entire Western intelligence effort, which was pretty big, was what you might call a minus advantage. We'd have been better off doing nothing.' Yet, incredibly, not one of the five was ever brought to justice. Burgess, Maclean and Philby all fled to Moscow. Blunt was allowed to keep his job – Surveyor of the Queen's Pictures – and his knighthood for 15 years after he confessed his treachery in 1964. And the fifth traitor, whose exposure must wait until his death, was also offered immunity from prosecution in return for information.

The master moles thrived, condemning hundreds of people to death, because the Establishment could forgive almost any behaviour as long as a chap had the right pedigree. Reliability revolved around parentage, schools, universities, clubs and regiments. All the super spies qualified for trust on those grounds.

Harold Adrian Russell Philby, nicknamed Kim, was the meticulous rather than brilliant son of an Arabian adventurer who had also been involved in British India. In 1929 Kim arrived at Trinity College, Cambridge, to read history and economics. A year later, Guy Francis de Moncy Burgess, the larger-than-life eccentric son of a naval commander, moved into rooms just down the corridor, studying history. And in 1931, Donald Maclean, the shy, clever son of a puritanical Liberal cabinet minister, arrived to read French.

Cambridge had changed since their fathers' days. The Depression brought disillusion. Jobs were scarce, even for people with degrees. The great hope for change, the Labour government, was voted out in 1931. The crisis of faith in capitalism went hand-in-hand with worries at the war clouds gathering over Europe. Britain seemed unwilling to stand up to the rising tide of fascism. Would it side with Nazi Germany against Russia? Anti-Fascist students later fought and died for the Republican cause in the Spanish Civil War. Others chose a more clandestine way to channel their disgust. Soviet recruiters were taking full advantage of students' anxious anger.

At Cambridge, Donald Maclean wrote an article in a magazine denouncing 'the whole crack-brained criminal mess' of capitalist society which was 'doomed to disappear'. Yet in 1935 he successfully passed entrance examinations for one of the pillars of capitalist society, the British Foreign Office, and was posted to the Paris embassy where he quickly established himself as one of the rising stars of the diplomatic profession.

At Cambridge, Guy Burgess organized a strike by college staff, and was prominent at demonstrations against war and high housing rents. But after a trip to Moscow in 1934, he too was in London seeking an institutional niche. When he failed in attempts to join Conservative Central Office and *The*

Cambridge University

Times, he pulled strings to become personal assistant to Conservative MP Jack Macnamara, and accompanied him on three trips to Hitler's Germany.

At Cambridge Kim Philby became a committed but discreet Communist. In 1934, he went to Vienna, and was an eye-witness to bitter bloodshed in the streets as the Austrian government tried to put down Socialist attempts to challenge the old order. He helped Communists escape what he saw as police persecution, and married his landlord's daughter, Alice Litzi Friedman, a Soviet spy, to help her flee as a British subject. But by 1936, he was attending meetings of the right-wing Anglo-German Fellowship in London, and editing its pro-Hitler magazine.

All three men were carefully cultivating conservative backgrounds, changing their image to bury a rebel past. All three were under orders to penetrate the Establishment as Soviet Trojan horses. And the Establishment clutched them to its heart.

In February 1937 Philby left for Spain to cover the civil war from the Franco side. At first as a freelance reporter, then as *The Times* special correspondent, he made a big impression with his accurate, impartial reporting. He also made important contacts with British intelligence. And since the Russians were backing the Republicans, he was able to feed Moscow with secrets from the opposition.

Soon after he arrived, Philby narrowly escaped death in a horrific incident which nearly saved Western spycatchers a 26-year nightmare. The car in which he was travelling was hit by a Russian-made shell. Three journalists with him died. Philby escaped with head wounds. Three months later came a solemn ceremony laced with irony. General Franco, the arch-Fascist Philby secretly opposed, proudly pinned on his chest the Red Cross of Military Merit. There was another wry confrontation when Philby returned to England in 1939. He was interviewed about his Spanish adventures on BBC Radio – by Guy Burgess.

Burgess, a brilliant conversationalist, was able to make friends with the rich and influential despite his outrageous drinking and blatant homosexuality. He was combining his work for Macnamara with a new job at the BBC, and both roles brought him important contacts, in Britain and in Europe. Winston Churchill gave him an autographed set of speeches. And as war approached, he became a secret courier of messages to French leader Edouard Daladier and Italian dictator Benito Mussolini when Neville Chamberlain, the British Prime Minister, tried to initiate new dialogues outside normal diplomatic channels in a desperate last-ditch bid for peace.

Apart from keeping the Russians informed of crucial developments, Burgess was using high society gossip and his European trips to ingratiate himself with British Intelligence. They paid him for each tip-off, and in January 1939, his devious diligence paid off. MI6 offered him a full-time staff job.

The secret service was hopelessly understaffed for war, and one of Burgess's tasks was to recruit men to make up the numbers. His hunting ground was the plush clubs and society parties of London's West End. In August 1940, a new man just back from reporting the war in France was introduced by Burgess. It was Kim Philby, who had separated from wife Litzi to cut his known Communist connections.

Philby's efficiency made a quick impression on spymasters more used to the plodding efforts of former members of the British police in India. He was given a key post in MI6's Iberian section, with orders to counter the Nazi spy threat in neutral Spain and Portugal, and protect vital Allied shipping in the Mediterranean and Atlantic. It was a job he did well – with one exception.

In 1943 top German army officers and the Abwehr secret service chief, Admiral Canaris, were said to be losing faith with Hitler and his Nazi henchmen. An MI6 man working under Philby wrote a paper which suggested exploiting the split to end the war before Germany was driven to unconditional surrender. If the ploy had worked, thousands of lives could have been saved, and Eastern Europe would have been spared Russian enslavement. But Philby stopped the paper circulating to those who might have followed it up. He knew Russia wanted Germany destroyed, and divided, unable ever again to threaten the Soviet Union.

When *The Times* asked if Philby might rejoin their staff, the editor was told it was impossible 'because his present work is so important and he performs it with such exceptional ability'. Philby, like Burgess and Maclean, had burrowed deep inside the Establishment citadel. And as the end of the war neared, the trio stood poised to wreak even more serious damage.

What does Kim Philby's son John, born in 1944, think of his father? Soon after visiting him in Moscow in 1975, he said: 'My father is nearly always described as a traitor, yet in no way was he a turn-coat. Neither was he even a double agent. At a very early age he made a conscious decision and he stuck by it. He believed he had a higher loyalty and for that he fought, often at very great cost to himself. It is said he betrayed a group of Albanian exiles backed by the West and parachuted into Albania in 1949. Probably this is true. But the men sent in were armed to the teeth. They were not there on a package holiday. Spying is a dirty business. In cold wars, as in hot wars, people get hurt.'

Philby Looks After His Friends

In August 1945 the newly-appointed Russian consul in Turkey approached British diplomats offering a potentially devastating deal. Konstantin Volkov, who claimed he was area head of Soviet intelligence, wanted £27,500 and asylum in the West. In return, he was prepared to reveal every detail of Russia's espionage operations in Turkey, plus the lowdown on how the Moscow spy network operated. And he would name three Russian agents working inside the British government, two in the Foreign Office and one in counter-espionage. It was too hot a potato for the diplomats in Istanbul to handle. They had to pass the offer to London, and Volkov agreed to wait 21 days for a decision.

Twenty days later a British intelligence official arrived in Turkey. Kim Philby apologized for the delay, blaming vacation arrangements. He waited a few days, but Volkov never made contact. Weeks after Philby returned to London, the reason for the defector's silence become clear. A Soviet military plane touched down unannounced at Istanbul airport. A car raced towards it across the tarmac. A heavily bandaged figure was lifted aboard the plane on a stretcher, and the aircraft took off again. Volkov had been betrayed by one of the Moscow moles he was seeking to unmask.

To the Kremlin's delight, MI6 had unwittingly appointed Philby head of espionage directed at Russia in 1944. By the end of the war, he had a staff of 100 working for him. But his treachery was making all their efforts meaningless. British agents sent behind the Iron Curtain were caught and shot. Russia's spies in British institutions had a highly-placed defender.

The two Foreign Office men Volkov would have named were Burgess and Maclean. The former had entered the diplomatic service via the press department. But by 1946 he was secretary and personal assistant to Hector McNeil, a friend from his BBC days, and now deputy Foreign Secretary. Burgess, privy to Tory secrets before the war, was now close to the heart of the new Labour administration. He accompanied McNeil on official visits to Paris and Brussels, was his aide at the Council of Foreign Ministers, and shared cabinet confidences.

Maclean was even better placed. In 1944, he had been appointed Head of Chancery at Britain's American embassy in Washington DC. Secret communiques between Prime Minister Churchill and Presidents Roosevelt and Truman crossed his desk, detailing war tactics and later the groundwork for the NATO alliance. And from February 1947, Maclean was secretary of the combined Policy Committee, dealing with classified atom bomb information from America, Britain and Canada. He knew who was doing what where, and how much uranium the Allies were buying. The Russians had scientists spying for them – one, Allan Nunn May, whose story will be told later, was a Cambridge contemporary of Maclean. From what the diplomat told them, they could work out exactly how many bombs the West was making. Maclean had another advantage. He was given a permanent pass which allowed him to enter the US Atomic Energy Commission headquarters unaccompanied. It was a privilege even the commander of the American atomic effort did not enjoy.

Both Burgess and Maclean were showing signs of strain under the burdens of their double lives. They were drinking with increasing ferocity, and making highly indiscreet comments about themselves and British policy. But instead of sacking them, the Foreign Office gave them new chances. When Maclean's anti-American stance became intolerable in Washington, he was 'promoted' to a top job in Cairo, where he had access to confidential dispatches from key embassies all over the world. When his drinking there became inexcusable – he was arrested by Egyptian police – he was whisked back to London, and given six months to sort himself out. Then he was appointed head of the American Desk at the Foreign Office, which gave him the chance to tell Moscow of America's crucial decision to limit involvement in the Korean War.

Burgess, too, lived a charmed life. He was removed from a Far East propaganda operation for being 'dirty, drunk and idle'. Recuperating in Gibraltar after a fall at a restaurant, he insulted and scandalized diplomats

An unnamed Cambridge contemporary of Guy Burgess confessed to *Daily Mail* reporters in 1979 that he had organized an underground group in the Bletchley area of Buckinghamshire during World War 2 while working for the Ministry of Food on emergency feeding plans. 'I was to lie low and be ready to organize resistance if the Germans invaded,' he said. 'I managed to gather a great deal of useful information. One of my sources was a comrade who was a ticket collector on trains. He used to listen to the conversations of girls on their way home from war jobs – they used to speak rather freely and he picked up a lot.'

and tourists alike with his unwary outbursts about homosexuality and politics. But as in Maclean's case, loutish behaviour was punished only by a change of scene. Burgess was posted to Washington as First Secretary in August 1950. It was a catastrophic appointment for Anglo-American relations. But it caused even more trouble for Kim Philby and the Russians.

Philby had reached the pinnacle of his espionage career, officially and unofficially, a year earlier. He preceded Burgess to Washington, as MI6 liaison man with the CIA. American agents who had learnt to respect Philby as a colleague in London during the war had no qualms about letting him in on every major operation. CIA director Bedell Smith often briefed him personally. And Philby pretended to be as puzzled as the Americans when a series of top operations turned sour.

The two agencies launched a major attempt to foment a revolution in Russian-influenced Albania in 1949. Exiled King Zog offered his battle-hardened royal guard, and other volunteers, as guerrilla fighters. But for three years, every attempt to infiltrate men into Albania by submarine or parachute ended in disaster. The Russians were always waiting with ambushes. They even knew the emergency radio drill when one captive Albanian tried to stop a follow-up party falling into the trap. The operation cost 300 Albanian lives.

The same thing happened when the CIA and MI6 muscled in on a modestly successful venture by dissident Ukrainians – smuggling arms into Soviet-run Ukraine, and literature out. Couriers began to go missing, and the flow of literature became Russian propaganda. After two disasters, both Britain and America fought shy of further meddling behind the Iron Curtain.

Philby was not only betraying infiltration operations and CIA agents all over the world; he was also able to tell Moscow how much the CIA knew of Soviet operations. And by 1949 the CIA thought it knew a lot. In a brilliant code-breaking operation, Russian messages taped during the war, while priority was given to German and Japanese intercepts, were finally

> **Official files on the defection to Moscow of Burgess and Maclean should have become available to public scrutiny late in 1981 under the 30-year rule on historic documents. But Mrs Thatcher's government held them back. Labour MP Stanley Newens commented: 'I suspect that details of the investigation into the defection would be embarrassing to people still alive. There are also people now dead whose reputations might have to be re-evaluated if the documents were published.'**

TV personality Malcolm Muggeridge worked under Kim Philby during his war-time service as an MI6 agent' 'I was always delighted to see him, I enjoyed his company,' he recalled years later. Once, when both were 'quite plastered' after a good dinner in Paris, they walked up and down in front of the Russian embassy in the Rue de Grenelle, discussing how they could penetrate it. Muggeridge also met Burgess at his Bentinck Street flat in London. He was with Blunt, and Muggeridge took an instant dislike to the 'comically pernickety and gentlemanly homosexual' art historian. He said: 'It is extraordinary for a brilliant art scholar like Blunt to be a devoted slave, to the point of betraying his country, to the most philistine government, aesthetically speaking, that has ever existed.'

unravelled. Fuchs, the Rosenbergs and Harry Gold, atom bomb spies whose exploits are covered later in this book, were all tracked down after the Soviet backlog was decoded, though the CIA invented or hinted at alternative methods of detection to try to keep their cypher triumph secret.

The Russians told Philby not to bother saving spies who had already served their purpose. But he sat on a report naming Bruno Pontecorvo, an Italian born nuclear scientist who later defected to the Soviet Union. And he also protected a high-level political spy code-named Homer. Philby was supposed to help to track him down from a field of 700 suspects. But he knew from the start who he was – Donald Maclean.

When Guy Burgess arrived in Washington, unkempt, unreliable and utterly unsuited to diplomacy, Philby surprisingly took him under his own roof for nearly a year. It was a mistake that almost cost his career when, in February 1951, he asked Burgess to run a vital errand.

Philby knew the net was closing in on Maclean in London. He was one of the final four Homer suspects. But the Russians could not allow him to be arrested. The ravages of spying, drinking and repressed guilt had left him unable to withstand interrogation. He would crack, putting at risk the espionage network so carefully built up over 20 years. It was also important for the Russians to prove to other moles that a spy in trouble could rely on help from Moscow. Maclean had to be spirited out of harm's way.

Burgess was a friend Maclean would trust. Though notorious for eccentricity, he was not suspected of spying. America was only too glad to see the back of Burgess, whose buffoonery was no longer a joke. But to ensure a plausible reason for departure, Burgess went driving in Virginia and was stopped three times for speeding. With him in the car was a well-known homosexual, which further enraged the Americans. Burgess sailed home on the liner *Queen Mary*.

He contacted Maclean early in May, and both men became aware of MI5 counter-espionage men trailing Maclean. But it seemed there was no rush to leave. Burgess plunged back into his social whirl, Maclean continued to provide the Russians with updates from the American Desk in Whitehall. Then, on the morning of Friday 25 May 1951, Foreign Secretary Herbert Morrison signed a paper authorizing the interrogation of Maclean.

The fateful Friday was Maclean's 38th birthday, and he allowed himself a leisurely lunch with friends during a routine office day. But Burgess had no time to relax. He was tipped off about the interrogation within minutes of the go-ahead being signed. Hastily, he told a friend he could not make a planned weekend trip to the Continent. In fact, he needed the friend's ticket for Maclean. He packed, hired a car, and drove to Maclean's house in Kent, arriving as Maclean returned from his office. They shared a meal with Maclean's wife Melinda, then drove to Southampton. As they boarded the 23.00 ferry to Europe, one of them called to a docker: 'Back on Monday.' But Burgess and Maclean were never to set foot in Britain again.

The diplomats' vanishing act puzzled the public. There was no mention of espionage for years, and even when the two men were at last paraded in public by the Soviet Union, in 1956, both claimed they were not spies, merely 'peace lovers' disillusioned with the West.

But a more enduring mystery was why Burgess fled with Maclean. Philby had specifically told him not to go, realizing his disappearance would focus suspicion on his friends, particularly friends who had shared their Washington homes with him. Had he panicked, knowing his Foreign Office career was over? Had he too broken under the strain of drink, debauchery and a double life? Or had Maclean refused to go alone to a cold, forbidding country where he knew no-one? Had the Russians decided they could not trust Maclean to make the journey on his own? The West has still not found a conclusive answer.

Burgess helped the Russians assess British political news and Maclean was given a desk job at the Soviet Foreign Office. But neither was really happy in his new homeland. Burgess, homesick and out of place in a puritanical country, died in 1963, when his drinking finally caught up with him. Maclean, who lost his wife to Kim Philby, lasted until 1983. His status as a top spy was confirmed in 1956, when the CIA is said to have seriously considered kidnapping him to find out exactly what secrets he had betrayed.

Meanwhile, in June 1951, the third man they left behind was fighting for his espionage life . . .

Philby's Flight
Spares British Blushes

Kim Philby was instantly suspected of aiding the Burgess-Maclean escape, just as he and the Russians expected. He was one of the few who had links with both men – he was in on the secrets of Maclean's surveillance, and Burgess had been his house-guest. Moscow was gambling on Philby's ability to bluff his way out of trouble. And the master spy justified that faith in a way even the Russians could hardly believe.

MI6 chief Sir Stewart Menzies summoned Philby to London for a clear-the-air confrontation. Many colleagues refused to accept that calm, capable, well-connected Kim could be a Moscow mole. But top officers in their counter-espionage counterpart, MI5, had no doubts. They were re-evaluating Philby's career record and asking awkward questions, particularly about the Volkov incident. CIA chiefs were also certain of his guilt. They told Menzies: sack Philby or we end all intelligence co-operation.

Philby was not escorted home, but he resisted the temptation to flee to Russia. His ice-cold, calculating brain needed to learn how much his bosses knew. He resigned from the Foreign Service – with a £4,000 golden handshake. His resignation meant he could no longer be posted abroad under diplomatic cover, but did not rule out other kinds of undercover work.

In June 1952, MI5 pressure resulted in a 'secret trial' for Philby. For three days, Helenus Milmo, a former secret agent who later became a judge, grilled him about his past in front of assessors. Philby stalled, using his lifelong stammer to disrupt the rhythm of cross-examination and give himself time to think. He denied everything while carefully analysing exactly what his interrogator knew. It was soon clear that MI5 had only circumstantial evidence which would never stand up in court without a confession. Philby was not prepared to make one, and the trial ended inconclusively.

Philby had been mentioned as a possible director of MI6 during his heyday in Washington. Now he tried a succession of less glamorous jobs. He went to Spain as a reporter for *The Observer* newspaper, worked for a while in the City of London, and even became a toothbrush salesman. It is also possible he was used from time to time by MI6. He was seen in Cyprus, mixing with Armenians exiled from their Iron Curtain homeland, and spotted by scientists at a lonely outpost on the Russo-Turkish border. Friends in the service helped him out when he was short of cash, even paying school fees for some of his five children by second wife Aileen. But he made no attempt to rebuild his career. He seemed to be waiting for something to happen. In September 1955, it did.

At long last, the government published a White Paper on the disappearance of Burgess and Maclean. It was a 4,000 word whitewash. One MP dismissed it as 'an insult to the intelligence of the country'. But an MI5 man, furious at the omission of Philby's name, decided to force the facts into the open another way. Nobody could call Philby a spy outside Parliament without receiving a writ for libel. But statements in the House of Commons carry privilege, allowing newspapers to report them, however libellous. So journalists approached by the MI5 man briefed opposition MP Marcus Lipton. He asked Tory Premier Sir Anthony Eden: 'Have you made up your mind to cover up at all costs the dubious third man activities of Mr Harold Philby, who was First Secretary at the Washington embassy a little time ago?' Philby's link with the two runaways was finally established. Publicity next day made a full Parliamentary debate inevitable.

Philby later claimed it was 'the happiest day of my life' when Lipton asked his question. And in the debate on 7 November, Foreign Minister Harold Macmillan – the man with overall responsibility for MI6 – told MPs: 'I have no reason to conclude that Mr Philby has at any time betrayed the interests of this country, or to identify him with the so-called third man, if indeed there was one.'

Knowing that such official blessing made it unsafe for anyone to repeat Lipton's accusations, Philby held a jaunty press conference three days later, building for himself the image of a wholly innocent man whose career had crashed because of misguided friendship for the no-good Burgess. Even Macmillan knew that was not true. He was scrupulously fair to Philby in Parliament because he knew he could not be proved guilty. But he ordered MI6 never to use Philby as an agent again. Astonishingly, the order was ignored. Whether through illogical loyalty to a friend, or to keep him in the fold where he could be watched, Philby was sent to Beirut, a crucial espionage centre in the Middle East, where the Russians were currying favour in Egypt, Syria and the Gulf states.

Philby was using a foreign correspondent job for both *The Observer* and the *Economist* magazine as his cover, and filed impressive stories from the Lebanese capital. But the CIA were keeping tabs on his movements. He was

> **Writer Goronwy Rees, an Army intelligence officer during World War 2, met Kim Philby. He said of him: 'There was in him a streak of cruelty, malice and brutality which was never far beneath the surface and made him, one suspects, positively enjoy his life of treachery and betrayal.'**

Papers discovered when MI5 men searched Guy Burgess's flat in 1951 led to the discovery of a mole in the British Treasury. But it was December 1979 before the public learned that John Cairncross had spied for the Russians after being recruited to the Communist party by his teacher at Cambridge in the 1930s – Anthony Blunt. Cairncross claimed he 'just let Burgess see some notes I had made, general summaries of discussions and that sort of thing'. In fact, the papers were comprehensive briefings on Britain's attitude to Hitler and assessments of whether war with Germany was likely – crucial information which led to Russia's two-year pact with the Nazis in 1939. After being unmasked in 1952, Cairncross went into exile in Rome, working for the United Nations Food and Agriculture Organization.

travelling far more than was reflected in his journalistic output.

In 1962, the American agency wiped out any lingering doubts MI6 held about Philby's guilt. The CIA sent over the detailed debriefing of a Russian defector, Anatoli Golitsin, who identified Philby as the man who tipped off Burgess and Maclean – and as the organizer of a KGB operation against Arab states in the late 1950s. At around the same time, a woman friend of Philby's second wife told MI6 he had admitted being a long-term Soviet agent.

Sir Dick White, MI6 chief since 1956, decided to send one of his agents, Nicholas Elliott to confront Philby in Beirut. But first he agreed with the Attorney-General, Sir John Hobson, that the spy could be offered immunity from prosecution in return for a full confession. Elliott arrived in Lebanon early in January 1963 – but according to espionage expert Chapman Pincher in his book *Their Trade is Treachery*, the KGB had beaten him to it. Yuri Modin, the Russian who ran Burgess and Maclean in London and organized their flight, had already alerted Philby to Elliott's visit and prepared an escape route for him. Philby could not defect before the interrogation because he would endanger the source who told the Russians about it.

Philby drank more heavily than usual in the weeks before Elliott's arrival. But he was sober when he met his former friend, and said: 'I was half expecting to see you.' Elliott told Philby there was new evidence against him. According to Pincher, Philby then began a careful confession, without even asking what the new evidence was. He said he was recruited by the Russians in Vienna in 1934, had sabotaged the Volkov, Albanian and Ukrainian operations, and sent Burgess to warn Maclean. But there were other misleading sections of the admission which, says Pincher, point to it being a KGB exercise to protect other Soviet moles in Britain. Philby signed a two-page typewritten resumé of his statement, and Elliott flew to America to check it with the CIA.

Ten days later, on 23 January, Philby and a female friend were on their way to a dinner party when Philby stopped the taxi and got out, saying he had to send a cable to London, and would join the party later. It was six months before he was seen again in public – in Moscow. And like Burgess and Maclean, he left behind more questions than answers.

The Russians knew MI6 wanted Philby back in London for more thorough questioning. Could they allow that, realizing that he was feeling the strain of nearly 30 years spying? Or did they arrange his getaway because, with his MI6 prospects completely blown, he was of more use to them in Moscow? Did they also know that the CIA, learning at last the full extent of Philby's treachery, had sent a team to Lebanon to assassinate him? And did MI6 connive at the escape, frightening Philby into defection? Certainly by 1963 the government, already embarrassed by a spate of spy trials, to be discussed later in this book, would be glad to forego the blushes of another. And MI6 would not have to explain publicly why it continued to employ a suspected Russian agent for 12 years, in direct contravention of orders.

Philby said on arrival in Russia that he had 'come home'. He soon settled to a new life as a senior KGB officer in the Moscow headquarters at 2, Dzerzhinsky Square. He was given the Order of the Red Banner and Russian citizenship, and helped himself to Melinda Maclean, who had followed her husband, Donald, into exile. Later he ditched her too and married a Russian girl. His only contact with Britain was a daily copy of *The Times* – a special privilege from the Kremlin, so he could keep up with the English cricket scores. Western intelligence agencies have detected his hand in the planning of some KGB offensives in Europe, notably an attempt to steal NATO secrets in 1968. In June 1979, he was spotted in Damascus, Syria – his first known excursion outside the Soviet Union in 16 years.

What drove Philby to a career which, at its zenith, doomed every Western spying mission, offensive and defensive, before it began? Was it a life-long, unsuspected Communist conviction which nevertheless did not stop him enjoying the full fruits of capitalist society? Was it a desire for adventure inherited from his father? The experts are undecided. And Philby the mystery man says only: 'Knowing what I did, I could not have done anything else.'

The Establishment took belated revenge on the insider who betrayed its trust by withdrawing his OBE and striking him off the membership list at London's Athenaeum club. Little did it realize that, for 44 years, it was harbouring another Russian spy who had climbed even higher up the ladder . . .

Anthony Blunt: Traitor on the Queen's Payroll

Anthony Blunt joined Russia's 'Cambridge Circus' of spies even before Donald Maclean. Guy Burgess, himself enlisted by Kim Philby, recruited his fellow homosexual in 1935. But it was November 1979 before he was publicly unmasked as a traitor by Prime Minister Margaret Thatcher. Though he had confessed to the espionage authorities 15 years earlier, he went unpunished. For the spy who betrayed His Majesty's forces during World War 2 was, by 1964, Sir Anthony Blunt, Surveyor of the Queen's Pictures. And in 1946 he had spared royal blushes with a delicate, top-secret mission to Germany.

Blunt preceded his fellow Soviet agents to Trinity College, arriving in 1926. The London vicar's son proved such a brilliant scholar that he was offered a teaching post, and was a Fellow of the college when Burgess reached Trinity. The two soon became friends, and Blunt readily agreed to Burgess's suggestion that he work for the Russians to fight the spread of Naziism. When his Soviet spymaster ordered Burgess to London, Blunt took over his task of spotting other talented students likely to join the cause.

By 1939 Blunt too was in London as deputy director of the prestigious Courtauld Institute of Art. When war broke out he volunteered for military intelligence. He was rejected because of his Marxist past. Astonishingly, he was then accepted by MI5 on the recommendation of an art chum. For the next five years he undermined the counter-espionage operations of Britain's secret services just as effectively as Kim Philby was wrecking MI6's overseas efforts. Blunt the spy had caught the spycatchers on the hop.

One of his first acts was to tell Moscow that, for seven years, someone in the office of Politburo member Anastas Mikoyan had been feeding information to MI5. The mole's supply of information stopped immediately. Then Blunt revealed that MI5 had bugged the HQ of the British Communist party. And he kept the Russians informed about the names and duties of every MI5 officer – he was even in charge of the surveillance roster for a time, able to tell Moscow exactly who was watching whom.

Later Blunt worked closely with Guy Burgess in operations against the neutral embassies in London. Burgess was recruiting Spanish, Portuguese and Scandinavian envoys as agents for MI5. Blunt was involved in the clandestine monitoring of diplomatic pouches and telephone messages. He was thus able to spot likely collaborators for MI5 – and the Russians. The two men met regularly in Blunt's rooms at the Courtauld Institute in Portman Square, preparing reports for their Soviet contact and providing secret documents for him to copy. Late in the war, these included plans for Operation Fortitude, a vital propaganda ploy to persuade the Germans that the D-Day landings would be at Pas-de-Calais, not the real target, Normandy. The Russians had an interest in prolonging the war on the Western Front – they could then grab more of Eastern Europe. Fortunately for thousands of Allied lives, they made no use of Blunt's information.

Unusually, the Russians let Blunt leave MI5 at the end of the war. Normally a spy infiltrated into such a useful position would be left in place until discovery loomed, and it was later surmised that Blunt was freed only because there was an equally effective mole in MI5 to provide the service the Kremlin required in the cold war years. But Blunt did not leave the service of Moscow. His new job, as Surveyor of Pictures for King George VI, was perfect cover for his activities as a courier. Nobody would suspect him of running messages for Soviet spies, collecting information and leaving money in secret hiding places for other agents, passing on titbits of information gleaned in casual chats with former MI5 colleagues. All of these tasks Blunt now performed. He became an indispensible back-up to Russia's front line agents. He even saved Philby's skin when Burgess and Maclean fled.

After the diplomats' disappearance in 1951, security forces wanted to inspect Burgess's London flat. Blunt had a key, and let them in. While they searched for incriminating evidence, Blunt noticed three letters implicating both Burgess and Philby in traitorous activities. He quietly pocketed them.

The Russians knew Blunt would be questioned after the disappearance of his former colleague Burgess, and they told him to defect. Blunt, delighted with his new post and prestige as Buckingham Palace adviser, declined, saying he was confident of surviving any interrogation. Again, the Russians let him have his way. And despite 11 MI5 grillings over the next 12 years, he lived up to his promise. He was even able to continue to run messages for the Soviets, helping to re-activate Philby in 1954, and visiting him in Beirut.

Then, in 1963, his luck ran out. A brilliant young American recruited by Moscow at Cambridge in the 1930s was offered an art consultancy job in Washington by President Kennedy. Though he turned it down, he took the opportunity to clear his conscience. He admitted providing the Russians with personal appraisals of American attitudes, and named Blunt as the 'known Soviet agent' who had enlisted him and others.

In April, 1964, Blunt was confronted with this information by MI5 interrogator Arthur Martin. Then he was told that the Attorney General Sir John Hobson, had authorized his immunity from prosecution if he confessed.

Anthony Blunt

Without knowing what Blunt had done, and forgetting the Attorney General's rider – immunity from prosecution only if he had stopped spying in 1945 when Russia was still an ally – MI5 had wiped Blunt's slate clean. Now he was able to confess, which he did, and name some people he had recruited. He was also able to give misleading information to protect others.

Why was immunity so readily given? It is true MI5 had no hard evidence on which to base a successful prosecution, and could justify allowing one spy off the hook if he led them to more. But no-one at that stage knew the enormity of Blunt's crimes which, if detected in war time, would have sent him to the gallows for treason. The real reason for the unpublished 'pardon' was Blunt's royal connections.

In 1946, Buckingham Palace asked MI5 to nominate a trustworthy volunteer for a delicate mission in Germany. Blunt was no longer on the secret service staff, but agreed to undertake the task. He never revealed what it entailed, but the following year, having accomplished it, he was presented with the Commander of the Royal Victorian Order award. The mission may also have been a factor in his knighthood, awarded in May, 1956. In January 1983, Chapman Pincher reported in the *Daily Express* that MI5 officers believed the task was to retrieve records of possibly embarrassing conversations between Hitler and the Duke of Windsor – the present Queen's uncle – during the Duke's visits to Berlin in 1937. Blunt next day denied the report, claiming, rather implausibly, that he merely collected letters Queen Victoria wrote to her daughter, Empress Frederick of Prussia. He did not explain why it was so vital to collect them so soon after the war, half a century after they were written.

Clearly, dragging the Royal Family into a spy trial in the early 1960s, when there were more than enough spy trials anyway, was not in anyone's interests. So while less significant Soviet agents like Vassall began 18 year jail

---

Philby, Burgess, Maclean and Blunt continued spying for the Russians even though they knew that in 1938, the Soviet agents who handled them, a Hungarian called Theo and a Czech named Otto, were recalled to Moscow and shot in one of Stalin's bloody purges. Theo and Otto were both 'illegals' – secret agents working on false passports and false identities in other countries. After 1938, the 'Cambridge Circus' spies were controlled by 'legals' – Soviet spies working under diplomatic cover from their embassy in London.

sentences, Blunt retained his Palace job, his prestige and his reputation until, in 1978, author Andrew Boyle published his book, *The Climate of Treason*. Blunt was not named, but his exploits were. And public opinion was so outraged at the new revelations in the Burgess, Maclean, Philby saga that Mrs Thatcher was forced to act and Blunt was finally, publicly unmasked. He died in March 1983, aged 76, unloved and unmourned, stripped of his titles and totally disgraced.

Blunt gave interrogators many names of other Russian agents, mainly minor and no longer operating, but he always denied there was a so-called Fifth Man in the 'Cambridge Circus'. According to Chapman Pincher, the security authorities know there was – and know who he is. In his book *Their Trade Is Treachery*, he reveals that the spy was recruited by Burgess and Philby in Cambridge after Philby returned from Vienna, that he hid his Communist convictions to gain work at a government defence station as a scientific civil servant, and that he knew two top Russian controllers, Yuri Modin and Sergei Kondrashev, who was sent to Britain specifically to handle the scientist and George Blake.

In 1966, when confronted with evidence about his Communist past and offered immunity from prosecution, he declined to confess. As he was near retirement, he was allowed to qualify for his pension on non-secret work. Exactly who he was, and the damage he did, will have to wait, according to Pincher, until death renders the libel laws irrelevant.

Chapter Three

World War Two Spies

Britain was blissfully unaware that five Soviet
superspies were safely tucked inside its defences
when a second world war against Germany was
formally declared on 3 September 1939.
Fortunately the Allies had enough excellent agents
of their own to glean the inside information which
helped defeat Hitler and his Nazi hordes.

Dark Days for MI6

Vernon Kell, the captain who almost single-handedly rounded up the Kaiser's spies in Britain in 1914, was still in charge of MI5 in 1939. He now was a major-general and had a staff of 6,000. And once again he showed he was on his toes, even though the government had been dithering trying to appease Hitler. On the day hostilities were announced, nearly 6,000 suspects were rounded up and interned. But the Germans had learned the lessons of 1914. On 8 November 1939, they struck a crippling blow against the European operations of Britain's other espionage arm, MI6.

The first months of war were strangely quiet on both sides of the Channel. Whitehall needed more time to prepare for fighting and Hitler still hoped to come to some arrangement with London, so Britain would stand aside while he achieved his dream of European domination. At the same time, some anti-Nazis in his hierarchy were in secret contact with the Foreign Office in London, discussing the possibilities of peace if Hitler could be overthrown. The Pope was one go-between in these delicate negotiations. Then, in October, British agents in Holland reported that two Germans wanted to discuss an anti-Hitler coup. MI6 chief Sir Stewart Menzies gave cautious approval for contact.

The Germans claimed to be Captain Schaemmel of the transport corps and Captain Hausmann, an army medic. The British agents, Major Richard Stevens and Captain Zigismund Payne Best, met them in Arnhem, and drove to Amsterdam for more talks. The Germans outlined the terms if Hitler was overthrown: the return of Austria, Poland and Czechoslovakia to their status before Nazi invasion and the restoration to Germany of colonies taken away by the 1918 peace treaty. After studying the proposals, London gave the go-ahead for a further meeting, at Venlo on the border between Germany and the Netherlands.

No one knew that one of the Germans was really the Nazi masterspy Walter Schellenberg who, only months earlier, had almost succeeded in an audacious scheme to kidnap the Duke and Duchess of Windsor, from a villa in Portugal. MI6 learned of the plot just in time, and was able to ensure that the Duke got away to his war-time post: governor of the Bahamas. Now Schellenberg was playing his anti-Nazi role on Hitler's orders, to try to discover whether Britain knew of any real plots against the Führer. He had won enough of MI6's trust to be given a radio set and a code to contact Britain in case of emergency. He played the agents Stevens and Best along by hinting that his boss, a High Command general, might be prepared to fly to England.

Menzies was wary. The terms discussed in Amsterdam were different from those mentioned at the secret Vatican talks. He told Stevens and Best to be careful. Then, unexpectedly, a crazed German carpenter tried to blow up Hitler during a meeting in a Munich beer cellar. The Nazi leader, however, left early, and the bomb went off after his departure, killing 6 and injuring 60. The furious Führer immediately blamed MI6, and ordered Schellenberg to abandon his subterfuge. Instead he was to kidnap the British agents and bring them to Berlin for interrogation.

Stevens, Best and a Dutch espionage man drove into a trap as they arrived outside the Venlo cafe set for their rendezvous. Three Mercedes cars suddenly smashed through the border barriers, packed with SS men. Shots were fired to keep Dutch frontier sentries at bay, and the agent with the two Britons was killed as he drew his pistol. Stevens and Best were handcuffed, bundled into one of the cars, and driven back across the border, straight to Berlin. There a delighted Hitler presented Iron Crosses to Schellenberg and his SS team.

The operation was decisive in more ways than one. Britain called off the Vatican talks, fearing its goodwill might be betrayed there as well. High-ranking Germans responsible for the peace feelers went to ground as the Gestapo stepped up its hunts for other plots. And MI6 lost a complete network patiently built up in Holland. Worse was to follow. In the spring of 1940, German armies swept through the Low Countries and France, establishing full control over them in 52 days. They seized papers from embassies giving more details of Allied spy operations. By the summer of 1940, an intelligence insider in London admitted after the war, 'We did not possess one single agent between the Balkans and the English Channel.'

For a year, British espionage was forced to concentrate purely on defence. A special section of MI6 was planning sabotage operations in the event of a Nazi invasion of England. MI5 continued to round up spies sent in to replace those interned. Their task was made easy by the poor quality of many of them. One, Karel Richter, was stopped near St Albans, Hertfordshire, after parachuting into a field. He had no satisfactory explanation for wearing three sets of underwear and two pairs of socks on a warm summer evening. Other spies were detected because of a brilliant counter-espionage scheme, code named Double-Cross.

Early in the war, MI5 arrested George Owens, a Welsh engineer provided with a radio by the German Abwehr, and asked to organize a fifth column to aid spies who arrived by air. Intelligence chiefs hit on the idea of allowing Owens to send messages as agreed – but with false information to deceive the Germans. The plan worked perfectly. Each time Berlin warned that a spy was on his way, the authorities were waiting. Offered the choice of hanging or cooperation, many decided discretion was the better part of valour.

By the end of the war, 39 agents were sending fake facts back to the Reich. One fooled the Nazis so well that they dropped a large amount of money for him to continue his good work, and awarded him an Iron Cross. Sir John Masterman, chairman of the Twenty (XX) Committee which controlled the operation, said: 'We actively ran and controlled the German espionage system in this country.' But that was a comment in 1945. In the gloomy days after Dunkirk, Britain's spymasters were not nearly so confident. Then another espionage deception worked wonders for morale ...

Rudolf Hess: the Man the Stars Betrayed

The world was stunned in May 1941, when top Nazi Rudolf Hess turned up unexpectedly in Scotland. And there was astonishment when it was learned that he flew there secretly because of forecasts in his horoscope. But according to writer Richard Deacon, there was an even more amazing explanation. In this book, *A History of British Secret Service*, he says Hitler's deputy was lured to Britain by an ingenious intelligence operation master-minded by Ian Fleming, creator of fictional superspy James Bond.

Fears of a Nazi invasion were still rife in London in late 1940. But Fleming, serving in Naval Intelligence, believed the 'defection' of an influential Reich leader would make an attack less likely. He studied dossiers on all Hitler's henchmen, and settled on the Deputy Führer as the most likely target for delicate deception. Hess was known to be eager for peace with Britain so Germany could concentrate on crushing Russia. He was also known to be a sucker for astrology.

Both sides waged a psychological stars war between 1939 and 1945. Paul Josef Goebbels' propaganda ministry in Berlin pumped out predictions in articles for newspapers at home and abroad, and naturally the forecasts were all favourable to Hitler. London responded with a secret service version of planetary influences in which the Führer was not so lucky. Cunningly faked editions of German magazines were smuggled into Berlin hinting at doom and despair for Nazi leaders. In Whitehall, the War Office was given regular reports of what astrologers might be telling Hitler from Louis de Wohl, a

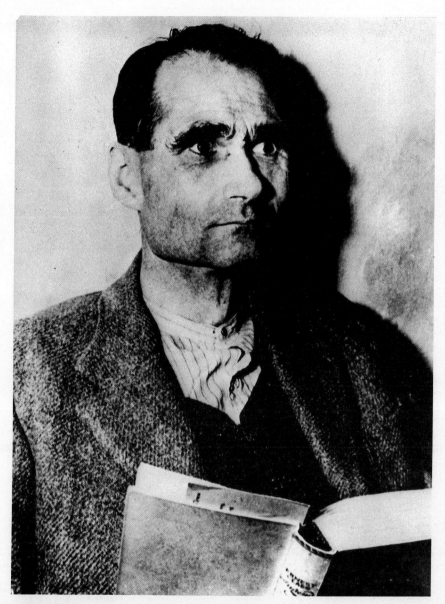

Rudolf Hess

refugee from the Nazis, who had learned the techniques of the Führer's favourite star-gazers. Hess also had a private predictions entourage, and it was this that the British set out to infiltrate and manipulate.

Fleming engineered the re-appearance of The Link, a pre-war Anglo-German friendship organization, in Lisbon and Tangier. He knew Hess had set up a spy network to rival Admiral Canaris's Abwehr, and that his men would rub shoulders with Allied agents in the two neutral capitals, both hotbeds of espionage. Soon Hess heard reports of influential Britons prepared to try to pave the way for a deal with the Reich. One of them was a Scottish landowner with royal connections.

Meanwhile sympathetic Swiss sources helped Fleming by placing an agent in Hess's astrological circle. Since he could report what 'genuine' forecasts the Deputy Führer was receiving, the task of fabricating predictions which suited Fleming's purpose was easier. And the agent could ensure that Hess identified the right Scottish landowner.

The name of the Duke of Hamilton had been carefully selected for the subterfuge. Enticing Hess with too prominent a personality was dangerous on two counts. His agents could check the possible contact out by quizzing neutral diplomats in London about his attitudes and behaviour. And if news leaked out in Britain that someone important had pro-German feelings, there might be public alarm. Hamilton, Lord Steward of the King's Household, had another advantage. He was serving in the RAF at a remote Scottish air-base close to his ancestral home. If Hess seriously undertook a clandestine peace mission, he would prefer to steer clear of the London spotlight and arrive unnoticed at a convenient landing strip.

A concerted astrological campaign began to build up. Fleming knew Hess would not take such a drastic step on the uncorroborated prediction of one man. Several fake forecasts had to be planted and brought to his attention. As luck would have it, there was an unusual configuration of planets at the end of April and the beginning of May in 1941. Hess was told this boded ill for Hitler. Then the possibilities of a quest for peace and travel abroad were worked into Hess's horoscopes. Independently, two astrologers told him 10 May was particularly significant.

That night, Hess flew a Messerschmitt 110 solo to Scotland. He ordered baffled police and Home Guard patrols to take him to the Duke of Hamilton. Instead he was arrested. But if Fleming expected his own government to rejoice at the news, he was mistaken. Though the Americans were enthusiastic, Winston Churchill and his aides were almost embarrassed. Possibly fearing a propaganda backlash about top Britons – even the exiled Duke of Windsor – backing Hitler, Whitehall went along with the official German reaction: that Hess was a lunatic.

But behind the scenes, Hitler took the incident as a devastating blow. Hundreds of people, many of them astrologers, were rounded up by the Gestapo and questioned about Hess's flight. And a month later, all public performances involving astrology, fortune-telling and telepathy were outlawed.

The Russians took Hess equally seriously. They never forgave the intent of his mission, to free the German armies for an assault on Moscow and vetoed all suggestions that Hess should be freed from his post-war incarceration in Berlin's Spandau Prison. The man who spent most of the war in a British cell was kept in solitary confinement long after all the other jailed Nazis sent to Spandau were released. Meanwhile, the British were enlisting the war help of a different kind of star ...

Hollywood Stars Take on Hitler

Famous names from stage, screen and radio signed up to fight the Nazi menace. Many took part in morale-boosting concerts for the troops. Singer Vera Lynn became 'the Forces Sweetheart' with her patriotic songs, and American bandleader Glenn Miller toured tirelessly until his mysterious death on a flight to France. Others made propaganda broadcasts from radio stations into occupied Europe to weaken the will to fight of German troops, and counter the disinformation pouring out of Berlin from the British traitor William Joyce, nicknamed Lord Haw-Haw. But many celebrities enlisted as espionage agents. David Niven, epitome of the English gentleman, was one of them.

Shortly after the star's death in July 1983, war-time colleague Ben Talbot talked of Niven's activities in the secret F squadron of the Special Air Service. 'He spoke fluent German and took part in raids behind the enemy lines' said Talbot. 'He was regarded as a first class agent who really put his life on the line. His job was to distract Luftwaffe base personnel while other agents sabotaged planes. He disguised himself as a German officer on many dangerous missions.' The British Defence Ministry confirmed that Niven served as commander of an undercover squadron in the Phantom Reconnaissance Regiment.

Jacques Cousteau, later to thrill the world with his breath-taking underwater films, was also an Allied secret agent against the Axis powers. In Sete, he photographed papers inside the Italian military headquarters which proved invaluable when the Allies invaded North Africa. Then, posing as a harmless diver, he roamed the Mediterranean coast noting Nazi naval movements. He was later awarded the Legion of Honour and Croix de Guerre.

In London authors like Malcolm Muggeridge and Graham Greene volunteered for intelligence work. Both worked for a time under Kim Philby in MI6, Muggeridge undertaking sensitive tasks in East Africa and Mozambique. John Le Carré, author of the 'Smiley' spy novels, also tasted undercover work at first hand. Historian Arnold Toynbee was responsible for daily reports to the War Cabinet on intelligence input, and novelist Dennis Wheatley was involved in planning the espionage coup of the *Man Who Never Was*, a story told later in this book.

But the most star-studded spy cast list belonged to William Stephenson. A film mogul in England before the war, Stephenson, on secret orders from Winston Churchill, founded British Security Coordination in New York to cooperate with American spy agencies. It was a delicate task for the man Churchill code-named 'Intrepid', for operations had to be kept secret from the US State Department, which was at that time determined to stay out of the war. But BSC grew into a major intelligence force, helped by some of Hollywood's biggest names.

Stephenson hired movie director John Ford to make propaganda films in Canada. The Korda brothers, Alexander and Zoltan, helped him build Camp X, a training centre 30 miles west of Toronto where espionage agents were given coaching for missions in occupied Europe. The Kordas recreated German locations for exercises and scoured film vaults for clips that could familiarize spies with their European destinations. Top Hollywood make-up artists were among those who helped agents with disguises, and other back-room staff were whisked to Canada to give acting lessons. Among the pilots who flew them there was Hughie Green, later a TV quizmaster and impresario in Britain.

Actor Leslie Howard, a star of the all-time box office smash hit *Gone With The Wind*, was on a secret mission for Stephenson when his plane was shot down over the Bay of Biscay in 1941. Noel Coward was another of Intrepid's travelling spies. As he toured the world, entertaining in night clubs in South America and Europe, he ridiculed intelligence work when in conversation with influential people who asked to be introduced to him. But he constantly reported all he heard and saw to Stephenson, and was able to fill in gaps in a jigsaw of anti-Nazi intelligence built up from other sources. Shortly before his death in 1973, Coward spoke for the first time about his spying. 'Everybody took me for a silly ass' he said. Since his face was so famous, and his manner so disinterested, no one suspected he could be an agent. Caught off-guard, they were often less than discreet.

Screen goddess Greta Garbo was also one of Stephenson's agents. Her contacts in her native Sweden were vital, and through her, Stephenson was able to check on German spies in Stockholm, set up escape routes for Allied escapees from occupied Europe, and order vital war supplies from an officially neutral country. When Churchill became alarmed at possible pro-Nazi sympathies within the Swedish royal family, Garbo and Stephenson were able to reassure him. In fact, Prince Carl Gustav Bernadotte was playing a vital spy role, to be outlined later in this book.

Stephenson's stars all played a big part in winning the war. But another of his agents, not known to the public, was to outshine every one of them . . .

Greta Garbo

Cynthia: the Spy They Couldn't Resist

The night-watchman at the French embassy in Washington was wary. He did not trust the couple who pleaded to be allowed to spend nights of passion inside the building. The man said he was married, and had nowhere else to pursue his affair. He always gave generous bribes. But two days earlier, the champagne with which they plied him had made him strangely drowsy. He had slept like a baby all night. Now they were back again. The watchman decided to check what they were really up to. He crept to the door of the room where they were. Gingerly he peeped inside – then backed away. The girl, a green-eyed, auburn-haired beauty, was completely naked, stretched seductively across a couch. Little did the guard at the Vichy French mission realize that his eyes had just feasted on the body of the most successful sex spy of World War 2, a woman whose espionage exploits made those of Mata Hari pale into insignificance.

Amy Elizabeth Thorpe was American-born, but had married British diplomat Arthur Pack during the 1930s. He was a dry, pompous man, completely unsuitable for a girl with her looks and spirit of adventure, but she stuck with him as his work took him to Chile, Spain and finally Poland. There she was at last given the chance of some excitement. In 1937, British intelligence invited her to become an agent. She accepted readily.

Soon Amy – codenamed Cynthia during the war – was the mistress of a well-placed official at the Polish Foreign Ministry in Warsaw. He told her of developments in Germany and Czechoslovakia, useful inside information for the British. But more important, she learned of Polish engineers working on a version of the German Enigma cypher machine. It was the first step in an operation which led to Britain acquiring the code which cracked Hitler's secret communications.

By 1941, Cynthia was in New York, the prize agent in the star-studded pack at British Security Coordination. William Stephenson needed someone to lure secrets from the embassies of the Italians and Vichy French. Cynthia's successes in Poland made her ideal. She was established in a comfortable home in Washington, and joined the cocktail party circuit in the American capital, renewing acquaintance with an old flame, Admiral Alberto Lais, now Mussolini's naval attaché in the USA.

Unlike later sex spies, Cynthia made no secret of her intentions. She blatantly told Lais she needed Italian codes and cyphers to help Allied intelligence in the war effort against his country. He was so besotted by her beauty that he provided them for copying. Even BSC veterans were stunned. One said: 'It seems fantastic that a man of his experience and seniority who was by instinct, training and conviction a patriotic officer, should have been so enfeebled by passion.' The Italian codes helped the outnumbered British fleet outwit Axis ships in the Mediterranean, and were of priceless value in the Allied invasions of North Africa. But once Lais had served his purpose, Cynthia threw him over. She told the FBI about his knowledge of sabotage in American ports, and he was sent home as an undesirable.

Her next target was the embassy of Vichy France, the pro-Nazi puppet government set up after Hitler's occupation of the country. Captain Charles Brousse, a former naval pilot, was the ambassador's press officer. He had worked with British intelligence before the war, but was sickened when British ships attacked the French navy at Oran in 1940 to prevent the fleet being used by the Germans. He was also no friend of Americans, believing them vulgar, with no understanding of the political realities of his country.

Slowly, seductively, Cynthia won him over. She was as smart mentally as she was attractive physically, and Brousse was captivated. He even agreed to her moving into the hotel where he lived with his third wife. He told her about a cache of French gold hidden on the Caribbean island of Martinique. BSC sent agents to locate it and prevent it falling into Nazi hands. Stephenson then cheekily used control of the gold as security in negotiations for badly-needed loans from America for the British war effort. Cynthia also learned of more Nazi plots against Allied shipping. And she was told of German agents in North and South America funded via the French legation. Then came a difficult order – get hold of new French naval codes.

These were locked in a strongroom at Vichy France's embassy in Washington. Even Brousse had no access to them. Together they planned

---

Wing-Commander Forest Frederick Yeo-Thomas was awarded the Military Cross and George Medal for his adventures with the British Special Operations Executive in occupied France. Once, ordered back to London when the German presence around Arras became too strong, he travelled to the plane pick-up point hidden under flowers in a funeral hearse, gripping a sten-gun to defend the secrets he was carrying home concealed in the coffin should German troops halt the cortège.

their love tryst deception of the night watchman. Generous tips and the 'nowhere to go' sob story made their faces familiar. Then came the night when they brought the bottles of champagne. The watchman's suspicions were correct. While he slept off drugs in the booze, Cynthia and Brousse let an expert locksmith in through a side door to study the vault where the codes were kept. And on the night the watchman peeped at naked Cynthia, BSC experts were at the vault copying the vital cyphers.

Like Cynthia's work on Enigma and the Italian codes, it was an espionage coup that changed the course of the war. In 1945, official BSC papers said the powerful and intoxicating hold Cynthia established over worldly wise men 'opened the way back into France and ultimately into Germany'. And when H. Montgomery Hyde, Stephenson's official biographer, asked Cynthia years later whether she was a little ashamed of her sexual antics, she replied: 'Ashamed? Not in the least. My superiors told me that my work saved thousands of British and American lives.'

Cynthia volunteered for further service in Europe. She wanted to be parachuted behind the German lines as a secret assassin. Though she had taken risks before, this time spymasters ruled it was too dangerous. After 1945, Brousse divorced his wife, and Cynthia's husband Arthur Pack was found shot dead in Argentina. He had been in poor health. The way was clear for Cynthia to marry Brousse, which she did. They lived in a castle in the South of France until 1963, when the world's most successful amorous agent died of cancer. Brousse died ten years later.

The Lucy Enigma

The Enigma machine to which superspy Cynthia alerted London was Hitler's answer to the success of Allied codebreakers in World War 1. He was determined nobody would undermine his military messages in the way Blinker Hall's Room 40 cryptographers deciphered the Kaiser's communications. Enigma was a machine which turned messages into unintelligible scrambles before transmitting them in Morse code. They could only be decoded by people possessing similar machines. After Cynthia's warning, British agents tried to find out more. Polish intelligence had men in the factories making them, and provided plenty of details. They even handed over a replica of the equipment. Then, in 1941, the Royal Navy captured the real thing from a German submarine. And British boffins built an equally ingenious machine – Ultra, an automatic decoder.

A special team, under Captain Edward Hastings, began furiously deciphering messages at a country house in Bletchley Park, Buckinghamshire. Station X provided a host of priceless intelligence. It enabled the Navy to find and destroy Nazi submarines faster than they could be replaced. It warned Montgomery of a trap set for his Eighth Army by Rommel after the Battle of Alamein. It helped in the sinking of the *Bismarck*. And it kept Allied commanders in touch with the latest battle plans of the Wehrmacht.

It was essential that news of the code-breaking was kept secret from Hitler. If he discovered that Enigma was compromised, he might switch to a new, impenetrable code. The Allies were thus forced to bite their lips even when they knew of imminent disasters. They knew, for instance, that German fighters would attack the plane carrying Leslie Howard on his secret mission for BSC chief William Stephenson. Luftwaffe orders had been intercepted. But to divert the plane would prove that eavesdropping was going on. Howard's death was unavoidable.

The secrets of Station X were only revealed after the war. And years later, espionage observers began linking its astonishing success with another of the great intelligence coups in the battle against Hitler – the Lucy Ring in Switzerland. It took its title from the code-name of Rudolf Roessler, a Bavarian anti-Nazi. Working with Englishman Alexander Foote and Hungarian Sandor Rado, he fed Stalin, the Russian leader, with amazingly accurate details of Hitler's planned invasion of the Soviet Union in 1941, and kept up a flow of vital facts for two years. Stalin knew in advance of every major Nazi tactic. But the information was so perfect that the Soviet supremo, himself a seasoned practitioner of cunning deceptions, started suspecting a German disinformation campaign. He eventually refused to trust the tips that were helping him win.

Roessler always claimed his data came from ten Bavarian anti-Nazis high in the German command, and it is probable that some of it did. But counter-intelligence by the Gestapo and Abwehr was never lax enough to allow almost daily, up-to-the-minute leakage of ultra-sensitive battle plans. Assessing Roessler's achievements, historians began looking for a plausible alternative source. And they settled with some certainty on Station X.

It was in Britain's interests to keep Hitler embroiled on the Eastern Front. Divisions bogged down there could not be used in western Europe. But spymasters realized Stalin would distrust information fed directly from London. They did not know then that he already had Philby, Burgess, Maclean and Blunt providing a service and the Allies dared not risk Stalin learning how they knew so much about Hitler's plans. The wily old fox might just betray Enigma to the Germans in a sudden peace pact. If the British facts came via Moscow's genuine network in Switzerland, it was reasoned, they might be put to good use.

The Lucy Ring continued its activities until late in 1943, when the Swiss, who turned a blind eye to what they called the *Rote Drei* (Red Three) while Hitler looked like swamping Europe, reverted to their neutral stance and rounded up the spies. The Abwehr had by then located the three transmitters sending German secrets to Moscow, and were threatening to act if the Swiss did not. The trio were given jail sentences of only a few months, then freed and deported.

Rado, the ringleader, was reluctant to return to Russia. He had defied orders not to share secrets with the Allies by telling Britain about lethal V2 rockets being built at Peenemünde. When Moscow did get its hands on him, there was no gratitude for the inside information which helped Stalin win the battles for Stalingrad and Kursk. Rado was sentenced to ten years in a Siberian prison camp. Only years later was his plight revealed by a former Soviet spy who was allowed to emigrate to Israel. He said that, on his way to Moscow, Rado contacted Maurice Oldfield, later a top British spymaster but then an agent in Cairo, and asked for asylum. His request was forwarded to London, but rejected. It had been sent to the desk of Kim Philby.

Roessler, possibly noting Rado's fate, never spoke about his sources. He died in 1958, taking the secrets to the grave. Foote was sent by Moscow to work in Mexico against the United States. But when he reached East Berlin he defected back to the British and took up a mundane civil service job in the Ministry of Agriculture in London, keeping quiet about his war-time experiences.

Czech spymaster General Frantisek Moravec went into the banking business to recruit spies before Hitler's invasion of his country. He opened banks along the border with Germany, and advertised loans to any soldier having trouble with creditors. The troopers could not believe their luck at the amazingly generous terms and sums offered. Then, when their debts got out of control, Moravec offered an easy way to wipe them out – espionage. The Prague intelligence chief also used Czech soldiers as spies. To disguise their military bearing he insisted on them always using walking sticks to cultivate a slovenly civilian walk.

The Mythical Major Martin

Rudolf Roessler and the Lucy Ring were not the only ace spies to find their secrets distrusted because they were too good to be true. Yugoslav agent Dusko Popov claimed in his autobiography that he gave full details about the Japanese raid on Pearl Harbour to FBI chief J. Edgar Hoover long before the devastating 'surprise' attack on 7 December 1941. And Hitler's Foreign Minister Joachim von Ribbentrop was guilty of just as great a blunder.

Elyesa Bazna was a Turk who decided to spy to raise money. He secured a job as a domestic servant in the British embassy in Ankara and began to watch the movements of ambassador Sir Hugh Knatchbull-Hugessen. Security was lax and Bazna decided to cash in. He won promotion to ambassador's valet and contacted the German embassy, offering secrets for sale. Using impressions of the ambassador's keys, Bazna could photograph sensitive documents left lying about his master's bedroom for perusal in the evening. They included a list of Allied agents working in Turkey, the minutes of military conferences, the diplomatic code, and plans for the invasion of Europe.

Local German spymasters, who codenamed the mercenary mole Cicero, sent the crucial information straight to von Ribbentrop in Berlin. He did not believe it possible for a servant to have access to such secrets. Germany's ambassador in Ankara, Franz von Papen, was told to ignore the source. But Cicero's contacts knew they were on to a good thing. They managed to persuade spy chiefs in Berlin to secretly provide more funds, and Cirero continued to deliver. Still the vain von Ribbentrop would not act on his intelligence.

In August 1943, a disillusioned German Foreign Ministry worker handed the first of nearly 3,000 documents over to American agents in Switzerland. They revealed Cicero's treachery. Somehow, news that his cover was blown reached Ankara, and the Germans tipped him off. He collected £300,000 hidden under his bedroom carpet and fled. Only later did he discover the cash the Nazis gave him was counterfeit.

While spurning genuine intelligence from Cicero, the Nazis fell for two espionage tricks by the Allies. And the results were to play a vital part in turning the war against Hitler. The fertile imagination of author Dennis Wheatley was involved in both.

> Abwehr spymaster Admiral Wilhelm Canaris was a
> cultivated man who viewed Nazi excesses with distaste.
> Many suspect he was behind the secret Vatican talks to try
> to find a peace formula at the start of the war. Attempts to
> contact him later were blocked by Kim Philby in London.
> Many Nazis hated Canaris. In 1944 they took their chance to
> humiliate him. When an Abwehr agent in Ankara, Turkey,
> defected to the British, Canaris was dismissed and his spy
> networks absorbed into the Gestapo. Then he was arrested.
> In April 1945, before the German surrender he was taken
> naked into the yard at Flossenberg prison and slowly
> strangled with piano wire, for the amusement of the SS.

At 04.30 on the misty morning of 30 April, 1943, the British submarine *Seraph* surfaced a mile off the mouth of the Huelva river on Spain's south coast. Crewmen struggled to bring on deck a bulky container marked 'optical instruments'. They opened it, and took a man's body from the dry ice preservative. An inflatable lifejacket was strapped to it and blown up. Then the body gently slid into the sea, followed by a rubber dinghy and paddles. The submarine submerged. The final step had been taken in the curious case of the Man Who Never Was.

A fisherman found the body later the same morning, and handed it over to a Spanish naval patrol. The British embassy in Madrid was informed of the tragic discovery, and given the personal effects of Royal Marine Major William Martin. They included an identity card, No 148228, £8 in notes, 5s 10d (29p) in coins, cigarettes, matches, a bunch of keys, two theatre ticket stubs and a receipt for a six-night stay at the Naval and Military Club in London's Piccadilly.

His pockets also contained two letters from a fiancée, a snapshot of her, and a bill for £53 for an engagement ring. There was a letter from her father in North Wales, less enthusiastic about the forthcoming marriage, a letter from Lloyds Bank demanding prompt action over a £79 overdraft and a note from some solicitors, confirming instructions for a will.

The embassy accepted the belongings while the body of Major Martin was buried with full military honours at Huelva. But a few days later British diplomats made alarmed protests to their officially neutral Spanish hosts. A vital attaché case Major Martin had been carrying was missing. The Spanish government promised to investigate. On 13 May the case was returned. Inside were important messages addressed to General Alexander, commander of the Eighth Army, revealing Allied plans to attack Cape Araxos in Greece, and to General Eisenhower and Sir Andrew Cunningham, Admiral of the Fleet. In the latter two letters, Admiral Lord Louis Mountbatten mentioned future campaigns and joked about sardines – a veiled reference to an assault on Sardinia.

In London, spy chiefs and scientists carefully examined the envelopes containing the messages. They discovered they had been opened. Through friends in Spain, the Nazis had learned the next targets of the Allied armies now in North Africa. Or had they? The German High Command were convinced they had. Forces were scattered in Greece and Sardinia to surprise the invaders. And when the full might of the Allies smashed ashore in Sicily on 10 July only one Italian and two German divisions were waiting. Losses on the beaches were light, and a path into Europe had been carved out quickly and efficiently.

Winston Churchill had said 'anybody but a damn fool' would expect the attack to be in Sicily. The mythical Major Martin made fools of the Germans.

Sir Winston Churchill

His mission to North Africa, and the supposed plane crash which deposited his body off Spain, were all figments of intelligence imagination. The meticulously detailed ploy had worked to perfection. But even in their moment of triumph, British spymasters kept their promise to the heartbroken parents who courageously gave permission for the body of their 30-year-old son, a civilian who had died of pneumonia, to be used in the scheme. His identity has never been revealed.

It was almost beyond belief that the Germans would fall for another espionage ploy before the D-Day invasions of Normandy, but they did. A whole programme of inspired leaks and diversionary plots was launched before the assault on the beaches. But Nazi papers scrutinized after the war revealed that attention was diverted from the actual date of attack when General Montgomery, leader of the British forces, was reported by spies to be in Gibraltar and North Africa. Former actor M. E. Clifton-James had just given the most effective performance of his life.

Another Allied agent played a vital role in helping to turn D-Day into a lasting triumph. But he had to pretend for much longer, and in far more dangerous circumstances ...

Eric Erickson: Oil Salesman Extraordinary

American spies monitoring German manoeuvres before the decisive Battle of the Rhine in 1945 stared in astonishment as Hitler's on-the-run army prepared for its last stand. Horses were pulling ammunition trucks to the front. And tanks were being dragged into position by oxen. It was final proof of the success of one of the most dangerous espionage exploits of the war. Businessman Eric Erickson had fooled the Nazi top brass for more than three years. Travelling freely through Germany, once on a pass personally provided by SS supremo Heinrich Himmler, he located and inspected vital oil and synthetic fuel refineries, then told Allied bombers the best way to destroy them. But his triumph was achieved at a tragic price. To maintain his cover, Erickson was forced to watch helplessly as a firing squad slaughtered the girl he loved.

Erickson, born in Brooklyn, New York, had become an international oil dealer and a Swedish citizen by the time war broke out. During his world-wide travels, he was often in Germany and had noticed with concern the rise of the Nazis. Then, over dinner in Stockholm with an old acquaintance, Laurence Steinhardt, the American ambassador to Russia, he was offered a way of hitting back. Steinhardt knew that, sooner or later, America would become embroiled in the fighting. Already its secret services were preparing for the day. But they needed information on the Nazi oil supply lifelines. Erickson, with fluent German, established contacts in the Reich and good reasons for going there on business, could provide it. Would he? Erickson quickly agreed to try.

For 18 frustrating months he carefully cultivated a new image. He alienated all his old friends by angrily denouncing their anti-Nazi opinions, often in public. He hung pictures of Hitler in his office and home. Gradually he built up contacts at the German Legation. As a final coup de grâce, he persuaded Prince Carl Gustav Bernadotte, nephew of King Gustav, to forfeit popularity in neutral Sweden by pretending to sympathize with the Nazis. The Prince, convinced that Erickson's mission might shorten the war, bravely agreed to dine with local German big-wigs and flatter their snobbish egos. In September 1941, Erickson was at last allowed a visa for a business trip to Germany, having overcome all distrust at his American origins. Only one other Swede knew he was playing a role – his new bride, Ingrid.

The Gestapo were waiting when his plane touched down at Berlin's Tempelhof airport, and Obersturmbannführer Baron Franz von Nordhoff gave him a severe grilling about his attitudes to Hitler, the Nazis, America and the possibility of a Nazified Sweden. The smooth-tongued spy eased his way out of every tight corner, and was allowed to continue with his tour, ostensibly to buy German oil for his country. He memorized everything that might prove useful to the Allies. He also recruited a network of 12 trusted old friends to provide him with information about the oil plants where they worked. It took time to convince them he was really working for the Americans, and was not a Nazi agent provocateur. Many demanded a slip of paper, signed by Erickson, to prove to the Allies after the war that they had helped the cause. Erickson knew that each document would be his death warrant if it fell into German hands, but he had no choice but to sign.

Erickson travelled from Berlin to Hamburg, and on to Halle and Hanover. He memorized the exact layout of refineries, production details, nearby landmarks, the site of anti-aircraft batteries and fighter plane airfields. And on his return to Sweden, he poured the detailed data into a Dictaphone tube provided by American agents. Soon the oil Erickson had bought in exchange for iron ore credits began to arrive. Unknown to the Nazis, some of it was

> **Secret American bomb-sights helped the Luftwaffe blitz London and other cities during the Battle of Britain. Blueprints were stolen by ardent Nazi Hermann Lang while he worked at the Norden engineering works in Long Island, and were handed to an Abwehr agent in America. Delighted Luftwaffe chief Marshal Hermann Goering gave Lang 10,000 marks. He was arrested after an FBI spy infiltrated the Nazi secret service in America, and jailed for 14 years in 1941. He returned to Bavaria in 1950.**

used to fuel British patrol boats which were running the German naval blockade of Scandinavia to collect Swedish ball-bearings and other precious parts needed in the war effort.

When the Japanese attack on Pearl Harbour brought America into the war officially, Erickson came under more severe pressure. Some of his relations in the US cut all connections with the 'Nazi-lover'. The Gestapo checked him out again, even taking the trouble to collect his records from Cornell University where he had taken an engineering degree in 1921. Once more he was able to set their minds at rest, and throughout 1942 he made several trips to Germany, sometimes with Prince Carl. He also began visiting countries under Nazi occupation, inspecting refineries commandeered for the Reich war effort. On 12 June his information was acted on for the first time. American B-24 bombers flew from Egypt to attack the vital oil base at Ploesti, Rumania. Thereafter the businessman-spy spent hours in air raid shelters during his trips to Germany as the US Eighth Air Force accurately blasted refineries in Hamburg, Hanover, Marienburg and Ludwigshafen. During the summer of 1943 177 heavy bombers attacked Ploesti again. Erickson and his network were able to report that they had knocked out more than 40 per cent of the plant's refining capacity.

Erickson was living on a knife-edge. Apart from the possibility of being killed by the planes his intelligence was guiding, there was the constant fear of betrayal to the Gestapo, either by one of his agents or by accident. A crisis blew up when Hamburg contact Otto Holtz, one of the men who demanded a potentially lethal slip of paper, died unexpectedly. Erickson had to fly to Germany and retrieve the evidence from the bank vault before the man's pro-Nazi widow or son found it. It took two nerve-racking days of tact and subterfuge.

There was little escape from the relentless pressure. Erickson dared not let himself relax for a moment. When forced to share rooms at crowded hotels with other travellers, he took pills to stay awake, afraid of giving himself away by talking in his sleep. Then, late in 1942, he met attractive brunette Marianne von Mollendorf, another secret Allied agent. He became a courier to smuggle her secrets out of Germany, and she advised him on oil contacts and political changes. At first they pretended to be lovers as cover for clandestine meetings. Later they no longer needed to pretend.

In May 1944 waves of Allied bombers began blitzing refineries throughout the Reich. German fighters sent up to fend them off were ruthlessly shot down, 2,500 in one month alone. As the Luftwaffe ran short of planes, Nazi oil production was cut by half and more than 100,000 men diverted to repair work. The damage was a significant factor in the success of the D-Day landings and the long haul to Berlin. But it also gave Erickson a problem. The Germans now had no surplus oil to sell to Sweden. The excuse for his business trips had vanished. Then he came up with a brilliant solution. Instead of buying oil, he would pose as a seller. He offered to build a synthetic fuel refinery in Sweden, safe from the bombers, to supply the creaking Nazi war machine.

German officials in Stockholm were impressed by the carefully forged dossier of plans and bogus pledges of financial backing from influential Swedes. They forwarded them to Berlin, and Erickson followed to wine and dine decision makers. It took time to convince them, and required several trips to the German capital. Late in 1944 he flew into Templehof again – and was whisked off to the worst moment of his life.

Gestapo men, waiting as usual, drove him away, but not to their massive grey HQ at 8 Prinz Albrechtstrasse. This time the destination was Moabat jail. Erickson was convinced his espionage had been discovered, and he knew, from past warnings, how the Nazis dealt with those who betrayed their trust. Gloomily, he watched from a cell window as a guard loaded a machine gun in

---

American cryptographers broke the Japanese Purple Code after the disaster of Pearl Harbour. In May 1942 it enabled them to gain revenge and turn the tide of war in the Pacific. Admiral Chester Nimitz learned of a planned Japanese invasion of an island codenamed AF. He was certain the target was Midway, but just to make sure, he ordered the commander there to radio HQ that he was running short of water. Three days later, Japanese radio traffic revealed the water shortage at their target, AF. When the attack came, American reinforcements inflicted a shattering defeat.

the prison courtyard. Then he was led out into the sunshine. With relief he saw he was just one of a group of foreign visitors privileged to witness some executions. But when the condemned prisoners were led out, his heart turned to stone. Among them was Marianne von Mollendorf.

Fury and fear fought within him. Did the Nazis know of their liaison? Would Marianne think he had betrayed her? Could he, even at this late stage, do anything to save her? Was this all a charade to trap him into incriminating action? Their eyes met, but Marianne showed no flicker of recognition. Erickson steeled himself, battling for self-control, as she stood proudly in line. He forced himself to watch as the machine gun cut her and the other prisoners to ribbons.

Erickson went through the motions in the days that followed. And before the end of the week he was granted an interview about the proposed Swedish refinery by SS chief Himmler himself. It was soon clear that the Reichführer was as mentally unstable as rumours suggested, but Erickson cautiously managed to persuade him of the need for a personal inspection of German synthetic fuel plants to establish exactly what would be required in Stockholm. He was given a pass which allowed unrestricted travel.

Erickson began his tour, but was quickly aware, despite Himmler's words, that the Gestapo were tailing him. It was important to let them do so. As a businessman he was not supposed to know about espionage techniques, but it meant adapting rendezvous tactics. Information had to be left in the form of seemingly innocent notes on restaurant tables, slipped to contacts at fleeting meetings on street corners, whispered in the darkened corridors of bordellos. Finally, in Leipzig, Erickson's luck ran out. He was recognized by Franz Schroeder, an ardent Nazi who remembered the Swede's pre-war, pro-Jewish attitude. Erickson took him for beers at a tavern to try to explain his change of heart, but he could see Schroeder was unimpressed. When they parted, Erickson knew the German would alert the Gestapo. He had to be silenced. But first the spy had to shake off his SS shadow.

Darting through a nearby hotel, he leapt into a taxi, flashed his authority from the Gestapo chief, and ordered the driver to take the road down which Schroeder had walked. He soon spotted his quarry, and paid off the taxi to follow on foot. Schroeder went into a telephone box, and Erickson crept closer. Sure enough, the German was phoning an SS friend about his suspicions. Before he could go into details, Erickson pounced, driving his pocket knife into the back of the man's head, and wresting the phone from him. Memories of Marianne's death flashed through his mind, strengthening his resolve, somehow hardening his heart against natural repugnance at killing for the first time. As the body slumped to the floor of the kiosk Erickson vanished into the shadows.

Convinced that it would not take his Gestapo shadow long to make a connection between the body and the man Erickson had met, the Swede cabled Prince Carl, using the code which signified an emergency. By return came a telegram saying Erickson's wife was seriously ill, and he should come to Stockholm immediately. Sending his apologies to Himmler, who was due to meet him again, Erickson took the first available flight out of Germany. His American controllers agreed he could risk no more trips. But already he had done enough.

Bombing raids continued to sap the strength of Hitler's forces. Now the chemical plants Erickson reconnoitred were targets. The Nazis retreated through Europe, abandoning tanks, trucks and jeeps to conserve fuel. The Luftwaffe cut back on training time for pilots and tests on aircraft engines for the same reason, with catastrophic results. And munitions factories using the by-products of the synthetic fuel process ran short of raw material for shells and bombs.

In Stockholm, Erickson and Ingrid devoured every report of Allied advances, and rejoiced on 7 May 1945 at the German surrender. But they remained outcasts for another month. Then the cream of Swedish society were invited to a party at the American embassy. As they sipped their cocktails, the guests of honour were announced – and in walked the Ericksons and Prince Carl. Gasps of shocked disgust soon turned to humble apologies as the truth behind their pro-Nazi stance was at last revealed. And within days newspapers throughout the world were hailing the secret heroes who had done so much to crush Hitler.

Chapter Four

Atom Bomb Spies

For most people in the West, the end of war in
Europe in 1945 was greeted with relief and
rejoicing. But for spies and spymasters, there was
no let-up. For a new kind of war against a new
enemy had already begun . . .

Dr Allan Nunn May: the Treacherous Scientist

Igor Sergeievitch Gouzenko was a worried man. After two years as principal cypher clerk to the military attaché at the Russian embassy in Ottawa, he was about to be recalled to Moscow, and he knew life there could not compare to the luxury and freedom he, his wife Svetlana and young son Andrei were enjoying in Canada. Gouzenko began secretly copying documents to earn asylum in his new country. Their contents were to shock the governments of Canada, Britain and the United States, and expose what was later described as the greatest treachery of the century – the atom bomb espionage of Klaus Fuchs, Allan Nunn May, and Julius and Ethel Rosenberg.

The race to develop the atom bomb had begun in 1938, when refugees from Nazi Germany revealed that chemist Otto Hahn had successfully released an immense amount of energy by splitting the nucleus of the uranium atom. Realizing the horrifying potential of such a weapon in Hitler's hands, the British Prime Minister instantly set up a priority research programme, and sent teams of commandos to Norway to destroy a hydro-electric plant producing heavy water, essential to A-bomb experiments and then under Nazi control. In 1942, Britain and America agreed to pool their scientific resources to speed up production of the deadliest weapon the world had seen, but, though Russia was by then an ally in the war, the two Western powers agreed, largely at Churchill's instigation, not to share their progress with the Kremlin.

On 16 July 1945, a blinding flash, a tremendous bang heard 200 miles (320 km) away, and a multi-coloured spume of cloud stretching 40,000 feet high above the desert at Alamogordo, New Mexico, signalled the success of the Anglo-American team. Less than a month later, on 6 August, an American bomber unleashed the new bomb on the Japanese city of Hiroshima. It killed 78,150 people, effectively ended the war in the Pacific, and was hailed by the American President, Harry Truman, as 'the greatest thing in history'.

The Allies' sense of triumph was shortlived. On 6 September, when British envoys in Ottawa were still planning a victory garden party, Igor Gouzenko, then 25, tried to hand over his documents. At first nobody wanted to know. The local newspaper declared them too hot to handle. Officials at the Justice and External Affairs Departments stalled him while alerting Prime Minister W. L. Mackenzie King. It was decided the risk of a diplomatic break with

Russia – then still considered a friend and ally by Canadians – outweighed the value of Gouzenko's information and the possible danger of returning him to the people he had tried to betray. Only after four Soviet security men were caught ransacking Gouzenko's flat were he and his family whisked into protective hiding and his revelations taken seriously. They showed that:

American Secretary of State Edward Stettinius had been surrounded by spies.

Soviet vice-consul Anatoli Yakovlev was running sophisticated espionage networks from New York, sending military secrets to the Kremlin, laundering money for European operations and controlling his agents in Washington via courier Elizabeth Bentley.

Canada had been infiltrated by at least 20 Soviet agents, including two cypher clerks, Emma Woikin at the Canadian External Affairs Department, and Kay Willsher at the British High Commission in Ottawa, who had access to all highly-sensitive messages. And, most crucially; two Britons working on the atomic bomb in North American research laboratories were Soviet agents, and had passed secret materials and calculations to the Russians.

The scope of the clandestine operations staggered the Canadians, who quickly passed news of the bombshell on to the White House and 10 Downing Street, by now occupied by Labour Premier Clement Attlee. Throughout the war Churchill had counselled against trusting Stalin and the Russians. Now he was proved right. Far from reciprocating friendship, it seemed the Soviets were preparing for a new war. While counter-espionage services in the three countries began checking out Gouzenko's leads, the three leaders, Mackenzie King, Truman and Attlee, agonized over a response. The atom bomb leaks were clearly the biggest eye-opener.

Gouzenko knew the scientific traitors only by the code-names Alek and Golia. Alek was readily identifiable, thanks to a telegram sent to Moscow by

Dr Allan Nunn May was released from Wakefield Prison on 29 December, 1952. The British Cabinet considered depriving him of remission his good behaviour had earned, and keeping him locked up until 1956. They feared he would take his expertise behind the Iron Curtain. But Nunn May had learned his lesson. He went back to Cambridge, where years earlier he had gained a brilliant double first degree, and researched metal fatigue until 1962, when he went to Africa to become professor of physics at Ghana University.

Clement Attlee

Gouzenko's embassy boss Colonel Nikolai Zabotin, ostensibly military attaché but really a Russian spymaster in Canada. It revealed that Alek was transferring to work in London at King's College in the Strand. Inquiries at the Montreal branch of the Atomic Energy Division research laboratories established that Dr Allan Nunn May, a British physicist who had flown west to join the Allied nuclear programme in January 1943 was moving to London.

Since the telegram also revealed details of pre-arranged meetings between Nunn May and a Russian courier in London, the authorities decided to let him take up his new job, in the hope of tracking down more Soviet agents. Nunn May was to be in front of the British Museum on 7 October, carrying a copy of *The Times* under his left arm. His contact, holding the magazine *Picture Post* in his left hand, would ask for the most direct route to the Strand, and the scientist would offer to show him, adding: 'Best regards from Mikel.'

In the event, Nunn May never kept his secret rendezvous. 'I decided to wash my hands of the whole business' he told interrogators later, but on 15 February 1946, he was picked up by Scotland Yard Special Branch men for questioning in a coordinated trans-Atlantic swoop on the spies Gouzenko unmasked. At first he denied everything. But when confronted by evidence of his links with Soviet agents, he confessed to providing information and uranium samples to the Russians in return for 'some dollars (I forget how many) and a bottle of whisky which I accepted against my will'. He added: 'The whole affair was extremely painful to me and I only embarked on it because I felt this was a contribution I could make to the safety of mankind. I certainly did not do it for gain.'

Nunn May's motives were outlined at length by his defence counsel, Gerald Gardiner KC – later the Lord Chancellor – during his trial at the Old Bailey in May 1946. He said that, like doctors, some scientists 'take the view, rightly or wrongly, that if they have discovered something of value to mankind, they are under an obligation to see that it is used for mankind, and not kept for any particular group of people'. In addition, said the barrister, when the acts were committed, in February 1945, the Russians 'were customarily referred to as allies, and no one at that date referred to them as enemies or potential enemies'.

But Mr Justice Oliver was having none of that. Dismissing the attempt to portray Nunn May as 'a man of honour who had only done what he believed to be right' he made it clear he agreed with the prosecution, led by Attorney-General Sir Hartley Shawcross, who described the whole affair as 'a somewhat squalid case' of a man who made himself more important than his country's laws and policy. The judge jailed the traitor for ten years, saying he had shown 'crass conceit and wickedness' in compromising 'one of the country's most precious secrets'.

Back in Canada, the Soviet spymasters had fled home to Moscow.

While the police rounded up and put on trial their quota of the people Gouzenko named, his wife came out of hiding to go into hospital to give birth to her second child, a girl. She was booked in as the wife of a Polish immigrant farmer, and visited each day by her devoted 'husband' – a Royal Canadian Mounted policeman who had taken lessons in the art of speaking fractured English.

Gouzenko, Svetlana and the two children were later settled, under an assumed name and under RCMP protection, in a Canadian home known only to a select few. Over the years he occasionally appeared on TV to comment on subsequent spy scandals, always covered by a hood to prevent identification. He also wrote two books based on his experiences. But long before they were published, the counter-intelligence net was closing in on the other scientist traitor, Golia. Professor Israel Halperin, identified by Gouzenko as a spy, was acquitted by a Canadian court. But in investigating him, government agents had discovered an interesting name in his address book . . . that of Klaus Fuchs.

Emil Klaus Julius Fuchs: the Nuclear Spy

Of all the atom spies, Emil Klaus Julius Fuchs is generally regarded as the most valuable to the Russians, and the most traitorous to the West. Accepting sanctuary in Britain after fleeing Nazi oppression in his native Germany, he betrayed those who trusted him by actually volunteering his services as a spy, then giving the Kremlin the secrets of how to make the atom bomb.

Fuchs, a brilliant but reticent nuclear scientist, was born on 29 December 1911 – eight months after Allan Nunn May – in the village of Russelsheim, near Darmstadt. His father was a Protestant pastor who later turned Quaker, and the boy's pious but poor upbringing led him to membership of the Communist party. At the University of Kiel, he was beaten up by Nazi Brownshirts for his beliefs.

On 27 February 1933, Hitler's agents burned down the German parliamentary building, the Reichstag, and named the Communists as culprits. It was the prelude to a vicious purge. Fuchs, in Berlin for a conference, immediately went underground, made his way to Paris, and then, using a cousin's girlfriend as his contact, got in touch with a Quaker family in Somerset. They invited him to England, where he was befriended by academics and allowed to continue his studies in mathematical physics at Bristol University free of charge. He was the perfect student, quick and conscientious, and after obtaining his doctorate at Edinburgh, he was awarded a research scholarship.

With the outbreak of war with Germany, Fuchs, like all aliens, came under close scrutiny. But when he appeared before a tribunal in Edinburgh in November 1939, he was cleared to continue his work. Exactly five years earlier, the German consul in Bristol had told the local chief constable Fuchs was a Communist. But since he had not joined the British Communist party, and was not involving himself in overt Communist activities, the report was dismissed as a Nazi attempt to discredit him.

By May 1940, however, the Nazis had invaded Holland and Belgium, and Fuchs was interned with other hitherto trusted aliens. He was shipped to Canada, and was lucky to survive – another boat with internees on board was sunk by a U-boat. While in a prisoner-of-war camp there, he received newspapers and magazines from Professor Israel Halperin, a friend of Fuchs'

Dr Klaus Fuchs

sister, then living in America. But by 1941, Fuchs was back in Britain, freed because of strings pulled by his friends, notably his Edinburgh professor, Max Born.

That May, Fuchs had to sign the Official Secrets Act. German-born Dr Rudolf Peierls, the mathematical physics professor at Birmingham University, offered him a poorly-paid secret job connected with the war. Fuchs again passed a security vetting because the German warning about his Communist past was ignored. Peierls and his wife took the newcomer under their own roof for 18 months, until he moved into lodgings. They were among the influential figures who backed his application for naturalisation, which was essential for top secret work of national importance. On 7 August 1942, Klaus Fuchs formally became a British citizen, swearing an oath of allegiance to King George VI.

But Fuchs knew that oath was worthless. So did his Soviet spymasters because the German refugee from Naziism had volunteered his services to Moscow soon after arriving in Birmingham. Through a friend in the British Communist Party, he had contacted 'Alexander' – Simon Davidovich Kremer, the military attaché's secretary at Russia's London embassy – and at several weekend rendezvous in the Kensington area, he handed over carbon copies of his official reports, and handwritten notes on subjects about which the Soviets wanted more information. Fuchs knew exactly what he was doing: he even rang the Russian embassy to check that 'Alexander' was not a British counter-espionage agent.

Later, a German-Jewish refugee codenamed Sonya was given all the latest data on Anglo-American progress over the atomic bomb. She was Ruth Kuczynski, a Russian spy working from Oxford. She and Fuchs met in country lanes outside Banbury. Then he was posted to America to continue the work of nuclear collaboration. Sonya gave him precise instructions for a meeting with a Soviet agent in New York.

Emma Woikin, jailed in Canada for 2½ years after being named by Russian defector Igor Gouzenko as a Soviet spy in the Canadian External Affairs Department, told a Royal Commission investigating Gouzenko's revelations that she passed on secrets via the lavatory at her dentist's surgery. She left documents concealed there when she had an appointment for treatment to her teeth. The secrets were collected by the chauffeur of the Ottawa spymaster Nikolai Zabotin.

> **Innocent men lost their jobs after the treachery of Klaus Fuchs was revealed. To tighten security, it was ordered that , in future, all civil servants with access to secret material had to be British born, preferably of British parents. Dr Boris Davison, who also worked at Harwell, had to quit because his parents were still behind the Iron Curtain, and could be used in an attempt to blackmail him.**

Fuchs was given automatic security clearance by the Americans – not to do so would 'insult our principal war ally', a spokesman said later – and began work on a gaseous diffusion plant. But one Saturday in January 1944, he made his way, as arranged, to a street on the lower East Side of the city, carrying a tennis ball. A man called Raymond was waiting for him, carrying a book with green binding and two pairs of gloves. It was the start of a relationship which was to give Moscow the means to catch up in the nuclear race.

'Raymond' was Swiss-Jew Heinrich Golodnitsky, who had taken the name Harry Gold when his parents arrived in America in 1914. Fuchs never learned his true identity, nor that he worked as a biochemist for the Philadelphia Sugar Company, nor that he was a vital link in the espionage chain supervised by the Russian vice-consul, Anatoli Yakovlev, the spymaster named by Gouzenko. But he did know what he told 'Raymond' was reaching the Russians. And he told him all he knew, including details of a bomb-producing plant near Knoxville, Tennessee, and plans for the actual construction of the uranium bomb. The secrets were handed over at furtive meetings all over the city.

Then, late in 1944, Fuchs failed to keep two appointments. He had been instructed to join Dr Robert Oppenheimer and his old Birmingham chief Dr Peierls at Los Alamos air base near Santa Fe, New Mexico, for final assembly and testing of the bomb.

But he had not had time to tell Gold, who now worried that something had gone wrong. After checking Fuchs' apartment, he called on Fuchs' sister, living at Cambridge, Massachusetts, and left his telephone number. It was January 1945 before Fuchs travelled north and rang Gold's number. But the news was worth waiting for. The scientist wrote down all he learned at Los Alamos, and disclosed a second type of A-bomb, using plutonium. Details of design, components and manufacture were included in the dossier, together with information on a new implosion lens which triggered the bomb by exploding inwards.

Estimates of the amount of time Russia's spies saved in developing the bomb vary from 18 months to 5 years. And the West can only guess at how much money was saved because Allan Nunn May, Klaus Fuchs, David Greenglass and other traitors obviated the need to explore alternative avenues in nuclear research. Russia exploded its first bomb in September, 1949, four years after the first American blasts. Britain, which had cooperated in producing the US weapon, and then been denied access to it by the McMahon Act, had to wait until 1952 for its initial explosion – even though it had paid the wages of two of the scientists whose knowledge saved Russia so much.

Gold arranged the next contact for June in Santa Fe. There, sitting in a car on the Castillo Bridge, Fuchs revealed that the first test was due next month, and he would be watching it. He refused Gold's offer of $1,500, saying he did not need money.

When the men next met, in September, America had successfully exploded the bomb at Alamogordo, and dropped others on Hiroshima and Nagasaki. Fuchs gave an eye-witness account of the test blast, admitting he had under-estimated the Allies' abilities to create the weapon in time to use it against the Japanese. He also passed on all he knew of the bombs dropped on the two cities – size, materials, how they were detonated.

Harry Gold now dropped out of Fuchs' life. The scientist applied for, and won, the job of chief of theoretical physics at Harwell, the British atomic research establishment. Fuchs had mixed feelings about going 'home'. He had heard of Allan Nunn May's arrest, and though there was no direct link between the men, counter-espionage was sure to be on the lookout for more spies. In addition, the British, not the Red Army, had taken Kiel, the town where Fuchs had been to university. Would they find the German records of his early Communist connections?

The McMahon Act, passed by isolationist American senators, had cut Britain off from sharing American nuclear information, and Harwell was set up to develop an independent atomic weapon. Fuchs threw himself into his new job, recruiting staff, setting up programmes, sitting on almost every committee, even representing Britain in 1947 at a conference in Washington to decide what nuclear knowledge could be made public, and what could not. Ironically, Fuchs, the man who had given all of it to the Russians, argued against releasing too much to Western audiences.

For more than a year, Fuchs made no contact with the Soviets and they did not bother him. He was now of only minor value to them and, as became clear later, they had other sources of information. Donald Maclean and Kim Philby were both still in Washington, and Maclean attended the 1947 conference as the British embassy's political advisor on atomic energy.

Early in 1947, however, Fuchs did re-establish his links with the Russians. In a North London public house, he accepted £100 in notes, the first time he had taken any money other than his expenses. It was, he said later, a formal act to bind him to the cause, and over the next few months he passed secrets about the new Windscale nuclear reactor plant in north-west England, and information about British development of the bomb.

But for the first time Fuchs was beginning to withhold some facts. He also failed to turn up for some meetings. He was suffering what he later described as 'a controlled schizophrenia', in which his Marxist philosophy and acquired isolation from society – essential for the successful spy – were at odds with the friendships he was forging with the 'decent people' at Harwell.

In October 1949, a month after American planes detected the first Soviet atomic bomb blast, Fuchs went to Harwell's security officer, Wing Commander Henry Arnold, with 'a personal problem'. His father had become professor of theology at Leipzig University, in the Russian zone of Germany. They could use him as a lever to extract information about Harwell. Should he, Fuchs, resign?

Arnold stalled, saying he was not competent to advise. Then he contacted Service chiefs in London, saying Fuchs was suffering a crisis of conscience, and might be ripe for interrogation. Unknown to Fuchs, America's FBI and the British MI5 and MI6 had realized his treachery two years earlier. The clues had come in 1947 at a United Nations discussion on controlling atomic energy, when Soviet delegates clearly knew American techniques and codes, and from an intercepted message from the Soviet embassy in Washington to Military Intelligence HQ in Moscow. This narrowed the field to a British scientist at Los Alamos. By checking the movements of all Britons there it was possible to establish the spy's identity – Fuchs. But there was no evidence which would stand up in court.

Arnold's report triggered the big attempt for a confession. William James Skardon, a persistent but patient interrogator who was later to quiz Kim Philby, was sent to Harwell to question Fuchs. For the first two meetings, Fuchs denied being in touch with Soviet officials in America. Then, at the third meeting on 13 January 1950, the scientist abruptly changed his story, and decided to confess 'to try to repair the damage I have done ... to make sure that Harwell will suffer as little as possible and to save my friends as much as possible of that part that was good in my relations with them.'

Skardon was astonished when Fuchs admitted spying for seven years. Nobody had realized the extent of his betrayal. And he was appalled when Fuchs told him he considered the worst thing he had done was to tell the Russians how to make the atomic bomb.

Long, painstakingly detailed debriefings followed, and on the basis of what he said, the FBI were able to arrest Harry Gold.

Fuchs signed his confession on 27 January and seemed to think that, having cleared his conscience, he could return to work at Harwell. The authorities had other plans. On 2 February he was lured back to London and arrested by Commander Leonard Burt of Scotland Yard. Like Allan Nunn May, he was charged under the Official Secrets Acts with communicating information which might be useful to an enemy, and remanded in custody.

The arrest caused a sensation on both sides of the Atlantic. At a committal hearing, Mr Christmas Humphreys, prosecuting for the Attorney General, described Fuchs as a unique Jekyll and Hyde character, saying:

'Half of his mind was beyond the reach of reason and the impact of facts, the other half lived in a world of normal relationships and friendships with his colleagues and human loyalty. The dual personality had been consciously and deliberately produced. He broke his mind in two.'

But if the packed No. 1 court at the Old Bailey expected to see some kind of monster in the dock, they were disappointed. The nondescript, bespectacled defendant pleaded guilty to four separate specimen breaches of the Official Secrets Act, and made a brief statement in which he thanked the court and the staff of Brixton Prison for fair treatment, and was ready to serve his sentence to atone for his crimes.

Lord Chief Justice Goddard glared unmercifully at him. Hinting that hanging would suit the offences – 'Your crime to me is only thinly differentiated from high treason ... but you are not tried for that offence' – he said:

'You took advantage of the privilege of asylum, which has always been the boast of this country to people persecuted in their own country for their political opinions. You betrayed the hospitality and protection given to you by the greatest treachery.'

One hour and twenty minutes after the trial began, Klaus Fuchs left court to start a 14 year jail sentence – the maximum penalty under the law on which he was charged – in Wormwood Scrubs. On 12 February 1951, the Home Secretary formally stripped him of his British nationality 'on grounds of disloyalty'. As a stateless person, he could not be deported when he left Wakefield jail on 22 June 1959, having served nine years and earned full remission for good behaviour, but he chose to leave the country, and was driven to London, and put on a plane to East Berlin.

The Russians had publicly denied any knowledge of Fuchs at the time of his arrest. Intelligence experts later speculated that the Kremlin had set him up for arrest, since his worth to them had fallen, and a big spy trial would embarrass both Britain and America, and jeopardize future cooperation in high-security areas. Now they welcomed him back, approved the granting of East German nationality, and installed him as £12,000-a-year deputy director of the East German Central Institute for Nuclear Physics at Rossendorf, near Dresden.

In September 1964, he took over as director ... when his boss, Professor Heinz Harwich, defected to America.

Julius and Ethel Rosenberg: Traitors or Victims?

Were Julius and Ethel Rosenberg, as they claimed, 'the first victims of American fascism', condemned to death by 'the most monstrous frame-up in the history of our country'? Or were they, as President Dwight Eisenhower declared, master spies who, 'by immeasurably increasing the chances of atomic war, may have condemned to death tens of millions of innocent people all over the world'? It is a controversy which even America's new Freedom of Information Act has so far failed to resolve conclusively.

The Rosenbergs went to the electric chair in New York State's Sing Sing Prison just after 20.00 on 19 June 1953. It was the first daylight execution anyone could remember, to avoid the Jewish Sabbath which began at sundown. It was the first execution of a woman for a federal offence since the death of Mary Surratt for complicity in the assassination of Abraham Lincoln in 1865. And it was the first – and only – peacetime execution of civilians in America for espionage. What had they done to earn such an unenviable place in history?

It was a time of national paranoia about Communists and Communism. A wave of hysteria, fuelled by the Igor Gouzenko revelations and spy trials, was spearheaded by the Senate Committee for Un-American Activities, later led by the notorious Joseph McCarthy. Reds were suspected under every bed, and careers, notably in Hollywood, were wrecked on the flimsiest of evidence of left-wing leanings. Better dead than red was the watchword of the witchhunt leaders. And woe betide anyone who refused to answer correctly the universal question: 'Are you now or have you ever been a Communist?'

Less publicly than McCarthy, but equally assiduously, J. Edgar Hoover, ambitious and powerful ruler of the FBI, was waging war on Communist sympathizers. Once in his hands, there was only one way a red could make life easier for himself – by unmasking more 'commies'. Since Gouzenko had revealed Russian vice-consul Anatoli Yakovlev as a spymaster in New York, the FBI had managed to turn his courier, Elizabeth Bentley, into an informer, and in the course of investigating one of her tip-offs, they interviewed Harry Gold. Three years later, on 23 May 1950, he was arrested in Philadelphia in connection with his contacts with Klaus Fuchs. Gold made no secret of the fact that he had spied for the Russians since the 1930s and began naming more names, hoping cooperation would make his punishment lighter.

He revealed that, when he went to New Mexico to meet Fuchs in June 1945, he also contacted an American soldier working at the Los Alamos base. The soldier was carrying half of a torn packet top from a Jello pack which matched the half Yakovlev gave Gold in New York. Gold had to say 'Julius sent me'. The soldier then gave him details of the A-bomb implosion lens Fuchs had told the Russians about, and Gold handed over $500.

Gold was able to identify the soldier, from photographs the FBI showed him, as David Greenglass. He and his wife Ruth were already under suspicion for Communist sympathies. Greenglass was then working at a Brooklyn engineering firm with Julius Rosenberg, the son of Russian immigrants, who had married Greenglass's sister, Ethel. The FBI knew Rosenberg had been discharged after five years service in the US Signals Corps for belonging to an illegal organization, the Communist party.

Greenglass was arrested on 16 June 1950, and under questioning by an assistant attorney, admitted not only handing secrets to Gold, but giving information and sketches about the A-bomb to his brother-in-law in New

---

> **Harry Gold, the Russian agent involved in both the Klaus Fuchs and Rosenberg spy operations, was jailed for 30 years in 1951, but released on parole in 1965. The Kremlin, delighted with his efforts on the Soviet Union's behalf, awarded him the Order of the Red Star. But he died in Philadelphia in 1972 before he could take advantage of one of the benefits the Order gave him ... free rides on the Moscow buses.**

Julius Rosenberg

York on two occasions in 1945. He said Rosenberg told him they would go to 'his friends' the Russians. He also revealed that, after Gold's arrest, Rosenberg had advised Greenglass and his wife to flee to Mexico, and offered money to help them go. Other associates of Rosenberg, including a former college friend Morton Sobell, had escaped there, said Greenglass.

Julius Rosenberg was arrested the following day, even though he told the FBI: 'I didn't know anything about the atomic bomb until it was dropped on Japan.' His wife Ethel was arrested six days later, and on 18 August Morton Sobell was held in Laredo, Texas. He was allegedly deported by the Mexicans, though there was a firm suspicion that FBI agents kidnapped him and brought him north of the border to restore him to US jurisdiction.

Greenglass, Gold, Sobell and the two Rosenbergs were indicted, along with Yakovlev – then back in Moscow – on espionage conspiracy charges. Only Gold and Greenglass pleaded guilty. Ruth Greenglass was not indicted, even though her husband claimed Rosenberg sent her to Los Alamos to persuade him to spy. The reasons for her exemption only became clear years later, when FBI papers on the case were released to the public. Greenglass's attorney, O. John Rogge, had done a deal. Greenglass agreed to testify against his brother-in-law as long as Ruth was given immunity, and as long as the prosecution recommended a sentence for him of less than five years. Needing positive evidence against Rosenberg, the authorities agreed.

At that stage, Greenglass's statements had not implicated Rosenberg's wife Ethel. Now both David and Ruth made new admissions, stating that when they gave information to Rosenberg, he handed it to Ethel to type up for the Russians. The significance of this was revealed later when a note written by FBI chief Hoover to Attorney General Howard McGrath came to light. It read: 'There is no question that if Julius Rosenberg would furnish details of his extensive espionage activities, it would be possible to proceed against other individuals. Proceeding against his wife might serve as a lever in this matter.'

The FBI knew from an intercepted Soviet radio message that a husband-and-wife team in New York were involved in espionage. Their surveillance of Rosenberg convinced them he was a vital part of the Russian spy ring. And though they knew that the Greenglasses had been committed Communist workers since their early 20s, they were prepared to allow them to go to court with a story of being lured into espionage by David's brother-in-law.

Apart from the Greenglasses, Harry Gold and Elizabeth Bentley, the prosecution had another witness, Jerome Eugene Tartakow. He befriended Rosenberg over games of chess in the New York House of Detention, where Rosenberg was held pending his trial. Tartakow, also a known Communist, claimed Rosenberg revealed details of his espionage, and how he had taken care of some friends when he realized 'he had played the game and lost'. Rosenberg took a liking to his new young friend, who was serving two years for car thefts, and after his release, got him a chauffeur's job with his defence attorney. Rosenberg realized too late that Tartakow was an FBI informer.

When the hearing against Gold, Greenglass, Sobell and the Rosenbergs began on 6 March 1951, Judge Irving Kaufman quickly made it plain that any evidence about Communist connections was very welcome, despite defence protests that such testimony was no proof of espionage. Greenglass and Gold repeated their versions of the atom secrets hand-overs, Elizabeth Bentley told of telephone calls from a man calling himself Julius, and an electronics engineer, Max Elitcher, admitted acting as a courier between Sobell and Rosenberg.

Royal Navy Sub-Lieutenant David James Bingham was the spy nagged into treachery. Beset by money worries and a fiercely ambitious wife, he agreed in February to her suggestion that he sell secrets to the Russians. Bingham, 31, a £1,843-a-year electronics expert on the anti-submarine frigate *Rothesay,* received £5,000 for telling Moscow in detail about the latest nuclear depth charges, six underwater sonar eyes – recognized as the most advanced submarine detectors in the world – and Naval and NATO tactics and strengths. He gave himself up on 31 August 1971, claiming his conscience was troubling him after being promoted to a hush-hush Anglo American torpedo project. In fact a day earlier, Russian spy Oleg Lyalin had defected, and Bingham knew the game was up for him and his spymaster, Russian embassy assistant naval attaché Lory Torfimovich Kuzmin. At Bingham's trial in Winchester during March 1972. Mr Justice Bridge denounced his 'monstrous betrayal' and Attorney General Sir Peter Rawlinson said he had sold secrets 'almost beyond price'. Bingham was jailed for 21 years, but served only 7, being released on parole. His wife Maureen, 34, who admitted; 'I nagged him into becoming a spy and the Russians gave us money like water' was imprisoned for $2\frac{1}{2}$ years. The couple divorced while in jail, and their four children were taken into local authority care.

Then Rosenberg took the stand. He denied any knowledge of espionage. When asked whether he was a Communist, he invoked the Fifth Amendment of the Constitution, refusing to answer 'on the grounds that it might incriminate me'. But he did admit to admiring Russian achievements, adding: 'I felt and still feel that they contributed a major share in destroying the Hitler beast who killed six million of my co-religionists, and I feel emotional about that.'

Ethel Rosenberg was equally vehement in denying any connection with espionage, and non-committal when Communist associations were aired. In his closing speech, the couple's attorney, Emanuel Bloch, urged the jury to believe his clients rather than the Greenglasses, who had 'put it over on the government'. He added:

'David Greenglass was willing to bury his sister and her husband to save his life. Not only are the Greenglasses self-confessed spies, they are mercenary spies. They'll do anything for money. Any man who will testify against his own flesh and blood, his own sister, is repulsive, revolting, and is violating every code of civilization that ever existed. He is lower than the lowest animal I have ever seen.'

It was all to no avail. The jury found both Rosenbergs and Morton Sobell guilty. Sobell was jailed for the maximum 30 years, with a recommendation against parole. Both the Rosenbergs were condemned to death. The judge told them:

'I consider your crime worse than murder. In murder a criminal kills only his victim. Your conduct in putting into the hands of the Russians the A-bomb years before our best scientists predicted Russia would perfect the bomb has already caused, in my opinion, the Communist aggression in Korea, with the resultant casualties exceeding 50,000 and who knows but that millions more innocent people may pay the price of your treason. Indeed, by your betrayal you have altered the course of history to the disadvantage of our country.'

The two Rosenbergs were taken down to separate cells below the courtroom. There followed an incredible interlude which stunned jailers and fellow prisoners alike. Ethel sang Puccini's aria from *Madame Butterfly*, 'One Fine Day He Shall Return'. As applause rang round the cells, Rosenberg requested another song from the same opera. Ethel sang it, and responded to shouts from other prisoners with more songs, ending with 'The Battle Hymn Of The Republic'.

Emanuel Bloch lodged appeals, telling Rosenberg: 'You are two straws buffeted about by the political winds.' All his efforts were rejected by the courts. Eminent Nobel prizewinners Harold Urey and Albert Einstein aired their doubts in letters to newspapers, saying there was evidence of a family feud between the Greenglasses and the Rosenbergs, and pointing out that, while Greenglass and Gold, who confessed to spying, were jailed for 15 years and 30 years respectively, the only defendants to consistently maintain their innocence had been condemned to die – on the testimony of people who stood to profit from such a verdict.

Three times the campaign to reprieve the Rosenbergs reached President Eisenhower. On 11 February 1953, rejecting petitions for a new trial, he said: 'By their act these two individuals have betrayed the cause of freedom for which free men are fighting and dying at this very hour.' On 16 June he met a delegation of clergymen representing 2,300 church ministers and rejected a petition for executive clemency, admitting in a letter to his son John, serving in Korea, that, although it 'goes against the grain to avoid interfering' when a woman's life was at stake, he considered Ethel the stronger partner in the spy partnership, and added that if he commuted her sentence alone, 'the Soviets would simply recruit their spies from among women from here on'.

Finally, as protests against the deaths reached a crescendo on the actual day of execution, the President issued this statement five hours before the couple were due to walk to the electric chair:

'I am not unmindful of the fact that this case has aroused grave misgivings both here and abroad in the minds of serious people. I can only say that, by immeasurably increasing the chances of atomic war, the Rosenbergs may have condemned to death tens of millions of innocent people all over the world. The execution of two human beings is a grave matter. But even graver is the thought of the millions of dead whose deaths may be directly attributable to what these spies have done.'

Throughout the two-year ordeal of appeals, as each fresh hope was raised and dashed, the Rosenbergs kept each other's spirits up with letters that included expressions of tender love and angry denials of any guilt. There were also poignant scenes when they were allowed visits by their children, Michael and Robert, who were aged eight and four respectively when their parents were sentenced. Rosenberg wrote that he 'broke down and cried like a baby

Dwight and Mamie Eisenhower

> **Giorgio Rinaldi and his wife Angela Maria used their skills as parachutists to spy for Russia. The Italian skydivers travelled throughout the NATO countries giving aerobatic displays, and during rehearsals often photographed secret missile sites or sensitive airport installations. After their arrest in 1967, 29 other Soviet spies in 7 countries were rounded up as a result of Giorgio's admissions.**

because of the children's deep hurt' after one such visit. Finally, after a second plea to the Supreme Court was rejected by five votes to four, the execution date was set for 18 June – the Rosenbergs' 14th wedding anniversary. In the event, the end was delayed by 24 hours.

There remained one way to avert the execution. It was spelled out to both Rosenbergs by James Bennett, federal director of the Bureau of Prisons, on behalf of the Attorney General, Herbert Brownell. Cooperate fully with the government, he said, and we have the basis to recommend clemency.

Ethel asked Bennett if he wanted her to concoct a pack of lies. Julius likened the 'cooperate or die' ultimatum to the rack and screw of medieval torture chambers. And, through his lawyer, he told the world:

'By asking us to repudiate the truth of our innocence, the government admits its own doubts concerning our guilt. We will not help to purify the foul record of a fraudulent conviction and a barbaric sentence ... History will record that we were victims of the most monstrous frame-up in the history of our country.'

A special telephone line to Sing-Sing was kept open right to the last, in case either of the Rosenbergs 'changed their minds'. It remained unused while Ethel wrote her final letters, telling her children: 'Always remember that we were innocent and could not wrong our conscience. We press you close and kiss you with all our strength.' To Emanuel Bloch, charged with guardianship of the children, she wrote: 'You did everything that could be done. We are the first victims of American fascism.'

Julius Rosenberg died first, a flicker of a smile on his lips as he stared calmly in front of him. He did not say a word. As Ethel walked to the electric chair, the rabbi accompanying her made one last plea: 'For the sake of the children who still need you, will you say something which can save you? Must this tragedy be completed?' She replied calmly: 'I have nothing to say. I am ready.' She was 37, her husband two years younger.

Their deaths did not end the agonizing over their guilt. David Greenglass, released in 1960 after serving less than two-thirds of his sentence, was reunited with Ruth. They changed their names to start a new life in anonymity. He stuck to the version of events he had given in court. The FBI also maintained their conviction that the Rosenbergs were major figures in a prime espionage ring whose activities extended far beyond the offences for which they were convicted.

Emanuel Bloch, who died of a heart attack 8 months after the executions aged 52, said at the emotional funeral: 'Insanity, irrationality, barbarism and murder seem to be a part of the feeling of those who rule us.'

Michael and Robert Rosenberg continued to campaign about the innocence of their parents in association with the National Committee to Reopen the Rosenberg Case, and in 1975 Robert wrote a book in which he saw the Watergate scandal under President Richard Nixon as a natural development from the 'showcase trial' of his parents, which he blamed on government abuse of power.

But perhaps writers Sol Stern and Ronald Radosh came closest to the truth of the Rosenberg affair when they wrote in *New Republic* in 1979 of FBI documents 'demonstrating that Ethel was included in the indictment only as a hostage against her husband; and that she was ultimately convicted on tainted evidence obtained at the eleventh hour. The purpose was to pressure her husband into revealing details of his post-war espionage work.'

A dirty trick? Perhaps but then, as we shall see, the intelligence services of the West are far from alone in employing them ...

Chapter Five

Cold War Spies

Atom bomb espionage opened the eyes of the
Western public to Russia's clandestine hostility. As
the tension of the Cold War increased, particularly
in the early 1960s, a succession of spectacular spy
scandals hit the headlines. Britain, America and
West Germany were among the worst-hit
countries. But the espionage triumphs were not
confined to one side of the Iron Curtain ...

Gordon Lonsdale and the Portland Ring

Harry Houghton had never done a day's spying in his life. Then, one afternoon in 1955, a man with a thick Polish accent rang him. The quietly-spoken caller said he had a message from Karytzia, and Houghton's heart missed a beat. The man suggested a meeting in a few days' time at Dulwich Art Gallery in south London, and Houghton readily agreed. It was a date that was to irrevocably change Harry's destiny and earn him a place in history ... as one of the Portland spy ring.

Karytzia ... the name brought memories flooding back for Houghton. He had met her in Warsaw soon after being posted there as a naval clerk in the British embassy in 1950. After 20 years in the Royal Navy, he was new to the ways of diplomats abroad, and expressed surprise at the way drink flowed so freely at parties in a Poland still struggling to recover from the shortage caused by war. 'If you don't make your pile here, you're a mug,' he was told by a colleague.

So Houghton joined the black marketeers. He was given the address of a company in England that specialized in supplying embassies, and cornered the market in the supply of coffee. Orders arrived in the diplomatic bag, avoiding customs searches and freight charges. Harry quickly made his pile, and he invested some of it romancing his Polish buyer, a dark-eyed, dark-haired beauty called Karytzia. When his wife, who he eventually divorced, returned to England, Karytzia took to visiting his flat in secret. He left a light in the window to show he was alone.

Then, in 1952, he was posted back to England to work at the ultra-secret Portland Underwater Weapons Research Establishment. The affair became just a dream, and Houghton, by now middle-aged and drinking quite heavily, settled for comfort rather than excitement. He got engaged to Ethel 'Bunty' Gee, a frumpish, middle-aged secretary at the base. They bought a house together, and were in the middle of decorating it when the crucial call arrived.

Strolling round the art gallery, pretending an interest in the pictures, the stranger gave Houghton a nasty shock. The Polish authorities knew all about his affair with Karytzia and their black market racket. The girl could be in serious trouble because she had shown herself to be 'politically unreliable'. Houghton could ensure she was treated leniently – by supplying information about the anti-submarine base.

He went home to Ethel, and between massive slugs of gin, concocted an almost-plausible explanation for the call and his meeting. Alex Johnson, an American naval attaché he knew in Warsaw, had turned up in London and was threatening to expose his black market past, which could mean jail. He would keep quiet only if Houghton told him what was going on at the base. The Americans feared the British were withholding facts about the latest developments. Ethel, having waited a lifetime for her man, knew she could not bear to lose him now. She agreed to help.

Houghton was provided with a Minox camera, small enough to pass as a cigarette lighter, to photograph documents in the office. There was a bigger and better camera for documents he could carry home. Instructions for meetings were relayed by a code of pinpricks on life assurance brochures posted to him.

Cover for clandestine meetings was simple for hard-drinking Houghton. What could be more natural than bar-room encounters? He would stand with a glass in one hand and a newspaper tucked under his other arm. His contact would ask if it was the evening paper, be told it was the morning edition, and then inquire about racing results. He would then head for the gents lavatory, and when Houghton followed minutes later, packages would change hands. On the first Saturday of each month, Houghton went to London to meet his main contact, 'Alex Johnson', and deliver secrets about the performance of nuclear submarines and details of anti-submarine warfare.

But Houghton was not a particularly efficient spy. In fact, he was lucky to get away with it as long as he did. Both his ex-wife and his Warsaw boss had reported him as a security risk, and when colleagues twice reported that he was taking documents home, he was switched to a less sensitive job.

His big spending also aroused suspicions. He matched businessmen and farmers round for round in local pubs, and was always part of the group of after-hours drinkers. He also drove a new car while most of his workmates had to settle for old bangers. The Russians were paying Houghton well for his help – too well. He stood out like a sore thumb when, in 1960, the CIA told British spycatchers that defector Michal Goleniewski, codenamed Sniper, a Polish intelligence officer with KGB connections, had named a British source of naval secrets as Huton.

Police began trailing the Portland clerk on his tours of south Dorset hostelries. He was spending more across the bar than he earned. They followed him to London to meet 'Alex Johnson'. The watchers identified him from his car registration number as Gordon Lonsdale, who was posing as a Canadian businessman hiring out juke boxes to pubs and clubs.

Both men were now put under round-the-clock scrutiny. MI5 needed evidence before an arrest, and were anxious to see if Houghton and Lonsdale would lead them to more spies. Special Branch men's wives were enlisted to ensure that the two targets did not become too familiar with the faces of trackers. Special directional microphones taped conversations involving the two men. A fleet of cars, and even helicopters, tailed Lonsdale round London.

An attaché case he deposited at a Marylebone bank was secretly examined by MI5 after Prime Minister Harold Macmillan spoke to the bank's chairman. It held espionage equipment, including a cigarette lighter with a hollow wooden base in which code pads were hidden. Agents moved into a Regents Park flat next to Lonsdale's, and monitored morse code messages from Moscow.

Lonsdale, who was also running an operation to filch secrets from the Holy Loch nuclear submarine base in Scotland, had given Houghton specific orders at their London meeting. He wanted to know all about Asdic, a new top-security underwater sonar detection system which enabled warships to spot enemy submarines. Houghton was no longer in a position to get such data. But Ethel was. She still had high-level clearance, and dealt with Asdic papers every day as a filing clerk in the drawing office.

It was a simple matter to shuffle seven green-covered pamphlets into a brown OHMS envelope. Ethel walked down the stairs with the envelope under her arm. Nobody noticed her. Few people ever had. She met Houghton in the car park. Next day they drove to London to deliver the documents to Lonsdale outside the Old Vic theatre, near Waterloo railway station. As the spymaster casually lifted a shopping basket containing the secrets from Ethel's arm, the crowd milling innocently along the street surrounded them. The passers-by were Special Branch men and their wives.

Minutes later, uniformed police were knocking on the door of a bungalow in a quiet, tree-lined street in the London suburb of Ruislip. They told the man who answered they were investigating a spate of burglaries in the area, and advising householders on security. The man invited the officers in. He was not surprised at their mission – his own home had been broken into twice in the past few weeks. He did not realize that, on both occasions, the 'burglars' had been Special Branch detectives.

The man was Peter Kroger who, with his wife Helen, had been a vital link in the spy ring while posing as a bookseller. Their activities were revealed when Lonsdale was trailed to their home. Inside it, detectives found a 22.5 m (74 ft) long radio aerial, stretching from the lounge to the loft, a powerful radio transmitter with control setting charts under a kitchen floor trapdoor, and other espionage gadgetry – a microdot behind a picture of two children, a flask with a secret compartment, a torch with a false battery. The Krogers had been beaming to the Kremlin secrets gathered by agents all over Britain.

The authorities hoped to net more of those agents by delaying announcing the 5 arrests for 48 hours, but the news leaked out. 'Heaven knows how many members of the Soviet spy gang took the tip and got out of England,' wrote George Wigg, the Labour Party's security chief, who was to become an increasing thorn in the side of the Macmillan government over the next three years as scandal followed scandal. Journalist and writer Chapman Pincher claims the arrests had to be brought forward because spycatchers learned Lonsdale and the Krogers planned to flee once they had the Asdic secrets. Lonsdale allegedly told interrogators: 'We did not think you would do it so quickly.'

At the trial later in 1961, Lonsdale at first claimed the Krogers were innocent. He merely dumped equipment at their house while they were away. But MI5 had checked their fingerprints with the CIA. These identified the couple as professional KGB spies who, as Morris and Lona Cohen, had narrowly escaped arrest years earlier in a massive American round-up of Russians. Lonsdale, too, was not what he seemed. Inquiries revealed he was KGB masterspy Konon Trofimovich Molody, and had assumed the identity of a Canadian who had died.

Lonsdale was jailed for 25 years, but freed in 1964 in exchange for Greville Wynne, a British businessman imprisoned in Moscow, whose story will be told later. The Soviet ringleader died in Russia in 1970. The Krogers followed him home in 1969 – released in return for Gerald Brooke, a British lecturer imprisoned by the Kremlin for distributing anti-Communist literature.

Only Harry Houghton and Ethel Gee were no longer of any use to the

---

Australia was rocked by a spy scandal when Vladimir Petrov, ostensibly a diplomat at Russia's embassy in Canberra, defected in April 1954, and revealed that he was head of KGB espionage Down Under. Petrov reached safety just in time, but his wife, also a career KGB officer, was bundled onto a Moscow-bound plane by two agents sent to take the couple home. She managed to claim asylum during a refuelling stop at Darwin. The Russians were so infuriated by the incidents that they broke off diplomatic relations, evacuating their embassy and leaving their affairs in the hands of the Swiss. And the Australian people were astounded when a Royal Commission into Petrov's evidence revealed a Kremlin attempt to undermine the government with locally-recruited spies. Three had been infiltrated into the office of the Labour opposition leader.

Russian spymasters. They served 10 years of their 15 year sentences before release in 1971. They married, changed their names, and settled down to a quiet, anonymous life. Houghton wrote his memoirs – not for money, he insisted, but to clear Ethel – and claimed Lonsdale was just an errand boy. The real ringleader was still at large in Britain.

He was wrong about Lonsdale. Like the Krogers, he was a priceless asset who could still help the KGB. And a last desperate attempt to warn Moscow that he was about to be picked up led to the final unmasking of another master spy whose exploits had been even more damaging to Britain and the West ... George Blake.

George Blake: Deadly Deceptions of a Double Agent

The British public was stunned in May 1961 when it was announced that a spy called George Blake had been jailed for 42 years. It was an astonishing long sentence compared to those imposed on Nunn May, Fuchs and the Portland spy ring. What had Blake done? The trial had been held in secret, in the interests of 'national security', and Prime Minister Harold Macmillan refused to divulge the facts of the case despite repeated attempts by the Labour opposition to raise the matter in Parliament. Eventually he agreed to a confidential briefing for three Labour Privy Councillors, so minds could be put at rest. But what he told them had the opposite effect.

Blake was born in Rotterdam in 1922, the son of Albert William Behar, an Egyptian Jew who held a British passport, and his Dutch wife. The teenage George Behar joined the Dutch Resistance to Nazi occupation, but was eventually forced to flee to Britain, where he enrolled in secret organizations to carry on the war against Germany, finally changing his name to Blake, and working as an intelligence officer with the Royal Navy Volunteer Reserve.

After the war he transferred to the Foreign Office, where his brilliance as a linguist was quickly recognized. The Fuchs case brought in new rules, insisting that all civil servants should be British born, but by then Blake was already in the fold, working as a vice consul – and MI6 agent – in Korea. He was captured by the Communists and held in a North Korean interrogation camp for some months. Later suggestions that he was brainwashed at this stage were contradicted by fellow prisoners, who said Blake stood up bravely to his jailers.

By 1953, he was in Berlin for MI6, with instructions to infiltrate the Soviet spy set-up in the city that was, throughout the 1950s, the frontline flashpoint of the cold war between East and West. For more than four years, London was satisfied with his work in the complex, confused, murky waters of double agent espionage. Naturally, to win the trust of the Russians, he had to provide certain secrets, but MI6 remained confident they were getting more than they were giving. In fact, they were being duped.

In 1961, the arrest of a German spy and the defection of a Pole both provided evidence, too late, that Blake had turned triple agent. The spy was then based in Beirut. Interception of his message to Moscow, warning that Gordon Lonsdale was about to be arrested, was the final proof MI6 needed. An agent was sent to Lebanon to discuss a new job for Blake in London. It was the technique used with Kim Philby two years later. Philby fled to Russia. Blake, presumably unaware he had been unmasked, returned to England – and arrest.

The Macmillan government tried to justify the secret trial on the grounds that agents betrayed by Blake were still being withdrawn from behind the Iron Curtain. In fact, by then, they had all been rounded up and either shot or imprisoned. More than 40 anti-Communist agents around the world had been compromised. There were more secret shocks in store for the Labour Privy Councillors – leader Hugh Gaitskell, deputy leader George Brown and ex-minister Emanuel 'Manny' Shinwell – as they were briefed by Mr Macmillan and his Cabinet Secretary Norman Brook.

In Berlin, Blake had photographed almost every secret document that crossed his desk and handed the snaps to the KGB. He had hidden in the office when it was locked by a security man for the lunch hour, and worked undisturbed. He had informed the Russians of the whereabouts of prominent East Germans who had defected to the West, allowing the KGB to kidnap them and whisk them back behind the Iron Curtain. And he had betrayed one of the West's most expensive and ambitious projects, Operation Gold.

This was a joint project between the CIA and MI6 to build a tunnel to tap East German and Russian messages in East Berlin. It was conceived in December 1953 and took three months to dig. It began on the site of a new radar station near a cemetery at Rudow, in the Western sector of Berlin, and stretched nearly 0.8 km ($\frac{1}{2}$ mile) under the barbed wire of the border, 7.3 m (24 ft) below street level.

Huge iron pipes, 2.1 m (7 ft) in diameter, linked large chambers containing monitoring equipment, a telephone exchange switchboard and an air-conditioning plant. Highly sophisticated microphones, amplifiers, tape-recorders, teleprinters and transformers made it possible for the American, British and German eavesdroppers to listen in to 400 conversations at any one time. Lines were tapped from East German government offices, the KGB HQ in Karlshorst and the Soviet Army command post, with links to Moscow and other Warsaw Pact capitals.

During the first winter, heat rising from the tunnel began to melt snow on the ground above. A refrigeration system was quickly installed along the ceiling, and work on de-coding messages carried on inside the electrically-sealed security doors of the clandestine chambers.

Then, on 22 April 1956, East German border guards and Soviet intelligence staff began digging above the eastern end of the tunnel. Alarms gave the eavesdroppers time to escape, but the Western secret services had to watch mortified as the Russians milked every ounce of propaganda out of their 'discovery', giving guided tours to an estimated 40,000 people.

In fact, the CIA had suspected for some months that the tunnel had been detected. Telecommunications traffic from the tapped offices had dropped dramatically. Their suspicions were confirmed after Blake's arrest. He later claimed that he told Moscow about the project as soon as it was given the go-ahead. Had the West been deliberately misled for nearly three years?

Blake's treason continued in the Middle East. In 1958, the Egyptians exposed the entire British spy network in the area. Some agents were arrested. Others under diplomatic cover in embassies had to be hurriedly withdrawn, and President Nasser threatened to name every spy over Cairo Radio. He never did, but it took years for a replacement network to be set up.

Nasser had no reason to love the British. Two years earlier, Prime Minister Anthony Eden had sent troops ashore in the Suez crisis, and there are suspicions that MI6 was involved at the time in a plot by Egyptian rebels to assassinate their leader – a plot that was never put into action. But the reason for the 1958 clear-out was not primarily revenge. The Kremlin was about to supply Nasser with arms, and did not want British spies around to report the fact. Thanks to Blake, they were not.

Were Blake's superiors at fault, allowing him to know too much? Critics of MI6, while acknowledging that a double agent has to sacrifice some secrets, say that to feed him too many vital ones makes him vulnerable to blackmail or torture if captured – and the spymasters culpable if he proves a traitor. Colonel Charles Gilson, head of the Russian section of MI6 on the Continent until about 1958, shot himself in Rome after retiring. Money problems were the official reason.

George Blake

Blake, who was second only to Kim Philby as MI6's most damaging traitor, served just a fraction of his 42 year sentence. On 22 October 1967, he kicked out a weakly-cemented window bar at Wormwood Scrubs Prison, London, and vanished, resurfacing soon afterwards in Moscow. Once again, the KGB had looked after one of their own – and he had had time to write an ironic farewell. It was Blake's job to look after administration in the prison canteen. On the day of his escape, he had entered all the expenses and income in the accounts ledger, then added a note of apology – he had not had time to add up the totals.

William Vassall: Auntie Vera at the Admiralty

William John Christopher Vassall, the British Admiralty spy jailed for 18 years in 1962, said after his release: 'Traitor is not a word I associate with myself. I was simply a victim of circumstances.' And he added: 'If the attitude towards homosexuality had been as tolerant then as it is today, I would not have acted as I did.'

In retirement, former Prime Minister Harold Macmillan could probably sympathize with those words. But at the time, the storm created by Vassall's conviction, and the inquiry into the security services which followed, only added to the seemingly-endless series of scandals which rocked his Tory government in the early 1960s. Only later was it seen that Vassall was different from George Blake, Gordon Lonsdale, Klaus Fuchs and Kim Philby. They were dedicated spies or misguided intellectuals, doing what they did for ideological reasons. Vassall was just a pathetic, frightened man forced to betray his country by a cunning, perfectly-sprung trap.

The 29-year-old vicar's son was quickly spotted by the Russians as a likely blackmail target when he arrived as a junior clerk at Britain's embassy in Moscow in 1954. The KGB had agents in the building working as doormen or interpreters, and watched carefully as the lonely, slightly effeminate newcomer was snubbed by class conscious diplomatic types who viewed his attempts to socialize as social climbing. There was a strict pecking order among the snobs, and they constantly reminded Vassall that minor officials had to keep to their station.

The KGB moved tentatively at first. They engineered a restaurant meeting with a lively, attractive girl. Vassall showed little interest. They tried again with a male companion. Vassall was clearly more keen on him. The KGB knew he could be snared. But for a year they left him alone, to settle into the job and become a trusted member of the embassy staff. He was befriended by Sigmund Mikhailski, one of the KGB men on the embassy staff, who provided tickets for the Bolshoi ballet and the opera, and introduced the lonely Briton to Russian friends, some of them homosexual.

During Vassall's second winter in Moscow, one of the new companions invited him to a party in a private apartment at the Hotel Berlin. Vodka, wine and brandy flowed freely until Vassall felt quite dizzy. He was led to a curtained recess, undressed, and laid on a divan. He was vaguely aware of other men undressing, of photographs being taken ...

Two months later, a Russian army officer on leave invited Vassall to his apartment in the city. There was instant mutual attraction, or so it seemed. The men were naked on the bed when the door burst open and two KGB officers entered the room. The army man quickly dressed and left without a word. Terrified and humiliated, Vassall was shown the photographs taken at the Hotel Berlin. He was told he had been followed since arriving in Moscow. He had committed a serious crime against Soviet law. However, no one need hear of it, if he was prepared to cooperate.

Vassall was trapped and he knew it. Exposure could lead to prison, in Moscow or London, where homosexuality was then still a criminal offence. There would also be social disgrace and a possible international incident. He meekly agreed to become a spy.

At first his new masters nursed him, asking for names and jobs about which they already knew, just to check his truthfulness. At Christmas, 1955, they gave him 2,000 roubles, about £50. More envelopes crammed with cash followed. He could no longer have second thoughts and confess. 'It was like a spider's web,' Vassall was to say later. 'It was done very, very cleverly. At no time could I have escaped. I just got more and more entangled.'

In July 1956 the Russian investment really began to pay off. Vassall returned to London as acting personal assistant to the deputy director of the Admiralty's Naval Intelligence Division. The files in his drab office in Horse Guards Parade, overlooking the garden of No 10 Downing Street, were packed with high-security information, and fresh intelligence crossed his desk every day.

Each evening, as the civil service army headed home to suburbia, Vassall would have something more to do. He never carried a briefcase – the KGB had told him not to, because the chance of being stopped in spot searches was greater. Instead he slipped secret documents between the pages of *The Times* newspaper that he always carried, neatly folded, under his arm.

Then the £14-a-week Whitehall clerk would take a taxi to his £10-a-week Dolphin Square flat in trendy Pimlico, adorned with expensive antiques. He would take a special paper knife from his desk drawer, insert it into a hidden slot in his bookcase, and slip open a concealed drawer. There was the miniature camera, bought with KGB money in the duty free shop at Rome airport, with which he recorded every item he thought of value to the Soviets.

It was not time-consuming work – the Russians rarely asked him for specific documents – and he had plenty of opportunity to cut a dash around town in his 19 Savile Row suits, enjoying evenings at the opera, and West End theatre, a quiet drink at his club, dinner with a few discreet friends, or a visit to one of the twilight clubs which catered for his kind.

At weekends he went 'off to the country', usually visiting elderly ladies who

William Vassall

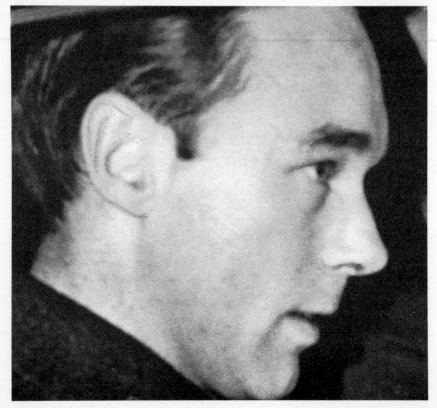

were enchanted by his fastidious charm, and thought he was 'something at the Foreign Office'. Vassall encouraged the air of mystery, dropping hints about legacies and private means to explain his apparent affluence. The same tactics worked at the office. The nickname Vera had followed him from Moscow, with Auntie added as a term of abuse. He was tolerated as a possible homosexual who kept himself to himself. Nobody really considered him a security risk.

Vassall was to describe his exploits later as 'not exciting, but terrifying'. And never more so than on the night he met his KGB contact, Gregory, at the King's Head public house in Harrow-on-the-Hill. After a few drinks in a quiet corner, Vassall went to fetch his coat, which had a spool of film in the pocket. His coat had gone, with a similar one left in its place.

Vassall tried not to panic. He left his name with the pub manager. Next day he telephoned. Yes, someone had called to say he had taken the wrong coat. Vassall dialled the number he was given. A man answered. He said he worked at Scotland Yard.

The reluctant spy walked to the Trafalgar Square rendezvous fearing arrest. He met the man he had spoken to on the phone. They exchanged pleasantries and coats, and parted. Vassall felt in his pocket. The precious film was still there.

When the Portland spy ring arrests hit the papers, Vassall met his contact on the Embankment by the House of Commons, and was told to stop operations. Nobody knew how much MI5 had learned from Lonsdale, Houghton, Gee and the Krogers. The Admiralty clerk treated himself to foreign holidays and invested in savings certificates and stock market shares. He was still picking up his KGB salary.

After a year, the Russians ordered him to start work again. By now, he had been promoted to assistant private secretary to the Civil Lord of the Admiralty, Thomas Galbraith, with access to the most recent developments in submarines and sonar detection. But Vassall's days were already numbered.

In December 1961, the American CIA had acquired an important defector in Helsinki, later revealed to be KGB Major Anatoli Golitsin. He was the man who brought conclusive proof of Kim Philby's treachery. And he also revealed that the Kremlin was receiving a steady flow of top quality British naval intelligence.

Armed with this information, it did not take long for the security services to narrow the field down to Vassall, still living above his visible means. Surveillance confirmed the suspicions. On 12 September 1962, Vassall prepared to leave his office to pick up currency for another holiday in Italy. Looking out of the window, he spotted an unfamiliar car in the official car park. Inside, three men were staring hard at the Horse Guards Parade entrance he always used.

He hurried to another way out of the building, but it was too late. 'There were more cars and more men with cold unkind faces,' he wrote later. 'They moved in on me. I was trapped.' But there were other emotions, too. 'It was the most wonderful relief,' he admitted. 'I hadn't the power or the strength to do it on my own. It wasn't exactly as if someone had come to help you. But it was what you had wanted to happen for such a long time.'

The trial, for recording secret official information useful to an enemy between 18 August 1956 and 11 September 1962, was a formality, and Vassall began an 18-year prison sentence. Then, in January 1963, a three-man Tribunal headed by Appeal Judge Lord Radcliffe began an investigation of the security aspects of the case. Newspaper reports had suggested that the existence of a spy in the Admiralty had been known for 18 months, since the Portland arrests, yet nothing was done. There were also suggestions of an over-friendly relationship between Vassall and his boss Galbraith.

The tribunal was able to give the lie to both allegations and clear both Galbraith and Lord Carrington, First Lord of the Admiralty, of negligence. But in the course of its hearings, two journalists were jailed for refusing to disclose their sources, ensuring that the embarrassing Vassall affair stayed in the front page headlines.

The spy himself was released on parole from Maidstone jail in 1972, and disappeared into the obscurity of a Sussex monastery under an assumed name. He re-surfaced briefly in 1980 when his story was shown in a television series on spies. He was remarkably philosophical about what had happened, saying: 'I don't hate anybody, even the KGB. They were just doing their job, and we have people like that too, don't we. What happened to me wasn't anything personal.' But he was bitter over one thing – how Anthony Blunt had been allowed to enjoy his freedom for 15 years after confessing his spying. Vassall said: 'I would like to lead my life the way he has been allowed to lead his.'

A KGB agent bugged the bed used by the British Queen during her tour of West Germany in 1965. Martin Margraf, who posed as a freelance waiter, was working at the luxurious Petersburg Hotel, beside the Rhine near Bonn, when the Queen and her husband, Prince Philip, arrived. He concealed a tiny microphone behind the headboard of their double bed, and retrieved it after they left.

Robert Lee Johnson: GI with a Grudge

Sergeant Robert Lee Johnson was one of life's misfits, a coarse, hard-drinking, gambling soldier. But the GI with a grudge was to provide Moscow with a rich harvest from seeds sown in unlikely ground and patiently nurtured for ten years.

Johnson was a military clerk with the US Army in Berlin in 1952. When passed over for promotion he developed an obsession to get even with his superiors. The best way, he decided, would be to defect to the Russians, and become a radio star, broadcasting propaganda to the West. But the Soviet officials he approached soon realized he was not the sort of citizen the Kremlin would welcome. They suggested another way to avenge his injustices – spying.

At first Johnson was enthusiastic. He photographed almost every paper he could find. The Russians, overwhelmed, asked him to desist, and instead suggested specific topics in which they were interested. Johnson, who had minimal security clearance, found such documents hard to come by. He lost interest in espionage, and when he transferred to a French posting of no interest to Moscow, the KGB ceased contact. In 1956, Johnson left the Army and returned to America. He lost what money he had gambling, and was living off the immoral earnings of the Viennese prostitute who had become his wife when, in January 1957, the Russians reactivated him. He was offered £150 a month for details about American rockets. Johnson applied to the Army and he was accepted at his old rank. He was posted as a guard to the Palos Verdes missile base in California.

Johnson pleased his KGB masters, providing drawings and photographs of missiles, overheard comments on their capabilities, and even a sample of rocket fuel. He continued to spy when transferred to a base at El Paso, Texas. Then he was sent overseas again, to Orléans in France. And there the Russians stepped up the pressure on their avenging soldier.

Johnson's wife had a nervous breakdown – the first of several – in 1960, and was admitted to an army hospital in Paris. Vitali Sergeevich Orzhurmov, Johnson's Soviet spymaster, suggested he apply for a job in the French capital on compassionate grounds. And in March 1961, he became a clerk-guard at the Orly airport Armed Forces Courier Centre.

This compact concrete bunker behind barbed wire in a remote corner of the airfield was closely guarded round the clock, every day of the year. It was one of the most sensitive mail clearing houses in the world. Vital military and diplomatic documents passing to and from Washington were delivered here. Orders and code changes to the US Mediterranean fleet and American Army bases, plus NATO up-dates on strategy for defending Europe, all passed through the bunker's steel vault, guarded by two steel doors. The Russians had long schemed how to have a look inside the 'impregnable' citadel of secrets. Now the unlikely Johnson was to be their passport.

A rule that French nationals could not be interrogated in US security clearance checks helped Johnson win the job. There was no major blemish on his past Army record, and officers appointed him, unaware that neighbours had heard Johnson's wife accuse him of espionage during their frequent and loud domestic disputes. Once their man was safely on the staff, the Russians questioned him closely on routine at the Centre. Johnson explained that the first door to the vault was secured by a metal bar with combination locks at either end. The inner door had a sophisticated lock opened by a key – but no one, not even a general, could open it unaccompanied.

Johnson was told to lie low and learn more about the vault without arousing suspicion. He volunteered to re-decorate the white-walled inner sanctum when the task came up, and was able to report that there was no secret alarm system inside. Months later, a young lieutenant momentarily left him alone as they sorted through a delivery to the vault, and Johnson took an impression of the inner door key in modelling clay the Russians had provided. He obtained the combination of one of the metal bar locks when a new officer carelessly wrote it down to memorize it, then discarded the scrap of paper in a wastepaper basket. But the other combination proved elusive.

Johnson now volunteered for all the unpopular overnight and weekend shifts, when only one man was left on guard. He explained that he needed midweek days free to visit his wife in hospital. The Russians gave him a Minox camera to take pictures of the combination lock from every angle. Later, they provided him with a circular metal plate and a metal cone 22.8 cm (9 in) long. He was to connect them either side of the lock, and stand clear for 30 minutes because the lock-picking computer was radio-active. Johnson completed the operation during his regular 18.00 hours Saturday to 06.00 hours Sunday duty. Three weeks later his Soviet controller handed him the necessary numbers to open the combination.

By now Orzhurmov had been joined in Paris by Feliks Aleksandrovich Ivanov, another diplomat who was really a KGB agent. The Johnson operation had become one of Moscow's top priorities, and they needed two men to ensure no unforeseen hitches. A routine was carefully rehearsed. Johnson was to take documents from the vault and deliver them to one of his

A British MP was charged with spying for an Iron Curtain country in 1970. Will Owen, 68 and Labour MP for Morpeth until he resigned his seat when charged, admitted receiving £2,300 from a man at the Czech embassy he knew to be a spy, in return for giving him confidential information he acquired as a member of the House of Commons Estimates Committee. Though acquitted by the jury, who argued that such information was not covered by the Official Secrets Act under which he was charged, Owen was ordered to pay £2,000 towards the cost of the trial. And Josef Frolik, the Czech defector who led MI5 to Owen, maintained the MP handed over secret military facts during a 15-year espionage career in which he was paid up to £500 a month. Owen died in April, 1981.

controllers on a lonely service road at 00.15 hours. He was to collect them again in a deserted lane near a cemetery 8 km (5 miles) away at 03.15 hours and replace them in the vault. If the overnight operation was undiscovered, he was to drop a Lucky Strike cigarette packet marked with an X by a telephone box on his way home.

The Russians had left nothing to chance. They showed Johnson two identical Air France flight bags. He was to deliver the documents in one, and receive in return the other containing a drugged bottle of Cognac and four antidote tablets. If anyone arrived unexpectedly at the Centre before his delivery or pick-up rendezvous, Johnson was to offer him a drink to knock him out for a few hours. If Johnson, too, was forced to drink from the doctored Cognac, the pills would prevent the drug affecting him. Johnson was also rehearsed in a getaway scheme should anything go wrong. Using a Canadian passport in his name, hidden along with money and instructions inside a hollow 'rock' in a field 16 km (10 miles) outside Paris, he was to flee to Brussels. He would be contacted there at Chaussée de Fôret using a recognition code based on identical 1921 American silver dollars.

Johnson first plundered the vault on 16 December 1962. It took him just two minutes to open the three locks and select a bagful of large manila envelopes bearing red and blue seals. A team of Russian specialists at the Soviet embassy in Paris, specially flown in via Algeria, carefully opened each one, copied the contents, and resealed them while Johnson sat at the Centre, watching the clock until his 03.15 replacement run. The plot worked perfectly, as did a re-run the following Sunday. And soon after Christmas, his Russian spymasters told him the Kremlin was so delighted with his efforts that he had been made a major in the Red Army, and given a US $2,000 bonus. Some of the most interesting documents had been read by Nikita Khruschev personally.

Flattered by such praise and appreciation, Johnson felt that at last he was really getting even with the Army. Now the vault was to be raided only at four to six week intervals, each time with the approval of the Politburo. This spy was too valuable to take any chances which might expose him to discovery.

To Moscow's consternation, things started to go wrong, despite the meticulous planning. At one 03.15 pick-up in February, Johnson's old Citroen car refused to start, and he and his Soviet contact spent 20 minutes making increasingly desperate attempts to get it going before succeeding. Johnson was given the money to buy a Mercedes. Then the whole escape network was alerted because Johnson forgot to drop his all-clear cigarette packet. It meant two days of writing explanatory reports for his long-suffering Russian minders. In April there was an even worse slip-up. Johnson fell asleep before the 03.15 rendezvous. Panic-stricken, Ivanov took the risk of driving to the Centre, and dropping the air flight bag packed with secrets in Johnson's car. The slovenly spy woke just in time, and was re-locking the last combination when his relief guard arrived.

Johnson told the Russians he was unable to get away because a courier arrived who refused his offer of the Cognac. But his spymasters knew he was lying. Couriers never arrived on Sunday mornings. They feared he had been detected and 'turned' by the Americans, so all operations were called off for the summer. Johnson was told it was because the nights were too short. In September, the vault plundering would begin again.

It did not, simply because Johnson was at last promoted and transferred, first to Seine Area Command HQ, then back to Washington, where his wife had been sent for further psychiatric treatment. The Russians hoped they could use him again later if he landed a posting in the Pentagon. But Johnson's unstable home life made that too impossible. In October, 1964, after yet another bitter row with his wife, he left their Arlington home for a gambling spree in Las Vegas. As an Army deserter, Johnson was investigated by the FBI. When agents questioned his wife, she accused Johnson of spying.

Johnson, who had surrendered to police, drunk and penniless, at Reno, Nevada, at first offered to become a counter-spy for the FBI. His offer was treated with contempt. Then he opened up with details of his espionage 'revenge' on America.

A Federal Court at Alexandria jailed him for 25 years on 30 July 1965. Johnson pleaded guilty, so the American public learned little of what he had done. Even US espionage experts could not estimate the exact extent of the damage he had caused. They had to assume the Russians might have seen every document that passed through Orly between 16 December 1962 and 21 April 1963. The Defence Department admitted: 'Our losses are enormous. Some are irreparable and incalculable. Had we not discovered the losses and had there been war, the damage might very well have proved fatal.'

Soon after the trial, authentic-looking US contingency plans began arriving at newspaper offices in Italy and Germany, purporting to show eventualities in which NATO would wage bacteriological and nuclear war against civilians in Western Europe and the Middle East. The scare reports were the more alarming because Johnson's theft of real documents had helped make the forgeries perfect.

At least four of the Soviet team involved in running Johnson received Russia's highest decoration, the Order of Lenin. But Johnson's story ended in the sordid fashion that he had lived his life. On 18 May, 1972, his son Robert, a Vietnam veteran, visited his 52-year-old father in Lewisburg Penitentiary, Pennsylvania, and plunged a knife into the spy's chest. Johnson died within an hour.

Guillaume: the Spy who Toppled the Chancellor

An audacious master spy forced the resignation of a world statesman in 1974. West German Chancellor Willy Brandt quit on 6 May, two weeks after it was revealed that Gunter Guillaume, his trusted aide for more than three years, was in the pay of East Germany's secret service.

Guillaume and his wife Christel arrived in West Germany in 1956, claiming to be political refugees from East Berlin. They settled in Frankfurt and both became members of the Social Democratic Party. Local workers were impressed by their commitment, and both were taken on the party staff, where their organizational ability quickly earned them responsible roles and influential friends. Patiently they ingratiated themselves until in 1969, they moved to the German capital, Bonn, first as aides to the Hesse State representatives, then on the staff of Herr Brandt at the Federal Chancellery.

Brandt was impressed with Gunter, both as a worker and a personal friend, and he soon became the Chancellor's personal assistant and confidante. In the summer of 1973, Guillaume was the only senior Chancellery official to accompany West Germany's leader and his family on a holiday at their lakeside cabin in Norway, and there he saw every sensitive teleprinter message sent from Bonn.

One was a letter from the American President, Richard Nixon, describing talks he had just completed with the French Foreign Minister. It revealed deep rifts within the NATO alliance which could prove dangerous if revealed to an enemy. Guillaume did just that, giving the secret information to his wife, a secretary in a state government office, who handed them to an East German courier.

Guillaume had worked as a photographer in East Germany until he was recruited as a spy, so he was expert at copying every high-security document which came his way. And once a month for 15 years, Christel delivered packages to a network of couriers. The secrets were often gift-wrapped, to look like presents.

But by late 1973, counter-intelligence officers from West Germany's secret service the BND, were on the couple's trail. It took nine months to pin them down, and on 24 April 1974 they were arrested at Bad Godesberg. The scandal rocked West Germany and stunned the NATO allies. Brandt's policy of a closer dialogue with Moscow was instantly questioned. And the

Chancellor, his credibility destroyed by the man he trusted to liaise with the party and trade unions, resigned.

The six month trial of the Guillaumes was held in a specially-built sound-proof cellar under Düsseldorf's State High Court. Much of the hearing was in secret, particularly when Herr Brandt was giving evidence. On 15 December 1975, Gunter was found guilty of treason and breach of official secrecy, and jailed for 13 years. He had refused to testify, and chewed sweets impassively as the five judges sentenced him. His wife Christel yawned as she was jailed for eight years for treason and complicity in betraying secrets.

The court cut two years from the sentences recommended by the prosecution, saying that the couple's treason was made easier by 'inadequate and belated control' of their activities by West Germany's spycatchers. And there were suggestions outside court that Herr Brandt might be prosecuted for negligence. In the event, the ruin of his career was considered punishment enough.

For 20 months after the couple's arrest, the East Germans made no mention of them. After sentencing, they applied for permission to visit the prisoners. And so began delicate negotiations for their release. Christel was freed first. She was exchanged for nine West Germans held in East Berlin in March 1981.

Gunter followed five months later, but the wrangling over the deal, and the terms of it, showed how highly he was valued by the Soviets. Top spy-broker Wolfgang Vogel, the man who swapped Peter and Helen Kroger for Gerald Brooke and U2 pilot Gary Powers for Soviet masterspy Rudolf Abel, was brought in to negotiate, and months of talks finally ended in an extraordinary exchange.

Guillaume, by then 54 and suffering from kidney trouble, was driven across the border in a caravan with curtains closed. Four other top Soviet agents were also freed, including Jorg Mayer, an East German spy arrested by Denmark in 1979, and Heinrich-Bernhard Zorn, another East German seized

> **Frank Bossard, an employee at the Ministry of Aviation jailed for 21 years in London in 1965 for passing secrets to the Russians, was finally trapped by minute electronic bleepers attached to sensitive files. Bossard was already under suspicion, but MI5 needed evidence to take him to court. When he took one of the bugged files out of the building, he was trailed to a hotel room, and caught in the act of photographing the aircraft secrets inside.**

in France in August 1980. Russia also wanted KGB major Alexei Koslov, jailed in South Africa following a West German tip-off, but the South Africans refused to join in the deal.

In return, West Germany received 35 of its nationals, held in East Germany for spying or helping people flee to the West, and 3,000 East Germans whose relatives had escaped across the Berlin Wall were allowed to be reunited with them. The Bonn government had to pay Deutchmarks worth £25 million as their passport to freedom.

By going home, Guillaume turned his back on a West German pension of £125 a week. He was entitled to it after paying into the state fund for 20 years as an employee. But there was consolation when he was reunited with wife Christel – he picked up nearly £40,000 in back pay from his grateful East German bosses.

Willy Brandt is not the only Western diplomat and politician brought down by the activities of Soviet bloc espionage agents. But, as the following section shows, the tactics are usually very different . . .

Defectors: Unexpected Bonuses

Western newspaper readers could be forgiven for thinking that Russia and her allies always win in the espionage war. Successive spy trials and scandals since 1945 have shaken public confidence in all NATO nations. But for every Western traitor unmasked, there are at least two defectors from Russia or her Warsaw Pact partners. Often the West's recruitment of a disillusioned Communist renegade or a carefully-cultivated double agent goes unpublicized for years, for good reason. The significance of what they reveal could be lost if the Soviet Union learns of the leaks, and takes precautions to guard its operations. And Russian defectors live in real fear for their lives. Moscow justice is usually meted out not by judges and juries, but by assassins.

Most defectors are minor agents of limited immediate value to Western spymasters. Their information about codes and how the KGB works forms part of a jigsaw which, when pieced together with facts from other sources, can lead to a breakthrough in the cold war. Others have priceless secrets to trade for asylum. And very occasionally, high-ranking Soviet intelligence officers betray their masters in a way which changes the balance of espionage power.

In 1953, the CIA recruited Lieutenant Colonel Yuri Popov in Moscow. For five years, until he was shot after betrayal by British traitor George Blake, Popov, an officer with GRU, the Soviet military intelligence organisation, gave the Americans the code names of nearly 400 Russian moles in the West. Many of them were identified and rounded up.

In 1960, another top man approached the West. Colonel Oleg Penkovsky said he turned traitor because he feared Russian leader Nikita Khruschev would plunge the world into nuclear war. He identified hundreds of Soviet agents abroad, including Eugene Ivanov, the spy in the Profumo affair. He handed over 5,000 documents about Russian military plans and weapons, especially rockets. He gave prior warning of the building of the Berlin Wall. But most important, he marked President Kennedy's card in the Cuban missiles crisis.

The world held its breath during October and November 1962, as the American and Russian leaders played what seemed to be a deadly game of brinkmanship. Khruschev had installed missiles in Communist Cuba, only 322 km (200 miles) from the American coast, and aimed at every major US city. Kennedy blockaded the island and demanded that the missiles be dismantled and removed. For days the battle of nerves seemed likely to unleash a third global war or even a nuclear holocaust. Then Moscow appeared to back down. The weapons were withdrawn in return for an American pledge not to attempt any repeat of the Bay of Pigs invasion adventure. What no one knew at the time was that Oleg Penkovsky had warned of the missile plan as early as April 1961, and kept Washington informed of Soviet decisions at every stage of the confrontation, giving Kennedy the confidence to make a tough stand.

Weeks later, Penkovsky and his British contact, Greville Wynne, were arrested. At a Moscow show trial early in 1963, the Russian was sentenced to death, and Wynne to eight years in prison. He served only 18 months before being exchanged, haggard and thin, for Gordon Lonsdale, mastermind of the Portland spy ring. Wynne claimed at his trial that he was an innocent businessman. But once safely back in Britain, he published two books bragging about his espionage exploits.

In one book, Wynne alleged that when Penkovsky came to England escorting a trade mission, he insisted on seeing the Queen and was introduced to Lord Mountbatten. The Russian also wanted to parade round London in a British uniform, and demanded £1,000 in cash to buy gifts for friends in Moscow. Such tales of bizarre behaviour helped raise doubts, not only about Wynne, but about Penkovsky. If the stories were true, how had the Russian survived as a spy for nearly two years?

In his book, *Inside Story*, published in 1978, espionage writer Chapman Pincher described Penkovsky as 'far more valuable (to the West) than Philby ever was to Moscow'. But by 1981, when Pincher published *Their Trade Is Treachery*, Penkovsky had become, 'in the minds of many members of MI5 ... a Soviet plant, the key figure in a disinformation exercise of the highest political consequence.' Now the suggestion was that Penkovsky was not shot. Nor, as Wynne claimed, did he commit suicide in his cell. Instead he was living in retirement, having fooled the West into believing that the Cuban missiles were important to Khruschev. In fact, according to the new thinking, the object of the crisis exercise was to protect Fidel Castro's Cuba as a centre for Communist subversion in South America – an object allegedly achieved by the American promise not to invade.

Such re-evaluations are not uncommon in espionage, where time can put a different perspective on events, where the borders between heroism and villainy are often blurred, and where suspicious minds are the first line of defence. The West has been conned by defectors who were not what they seemed. But in Penkovsky's case, the repercussions in Moscow after his arrest point to him being a genuine Western coup. General Ivan Serov, appointed GRU chief after the Popov affair, was axed along with several top assistants,

A disgruntled Soviet defector betrayed a Russian masterspy in 1955. Rudolf Abel, a KGB colonel with more than 30 years experience, arrived in New York in 1948 to build a replacement network for the Yakovlev spy ring blown by Igor Gouzenko. He established himself in Brooklyn as Emil R. Goldfus, an artist, photographer and radio enthusiast, and quickly impressed Moscow with his flow of secrets on nuclear weapons and rockets. In 1954, the Kremlin sent Reino Hayhanen to America to help with communications. But the newcomer was a reluctant spy and an alcoholic. Tired of his moaning, and afraid it would lead to a security breach, Abel arranged for Hayhanen's recall. But the espionage assistant defected rather than face the wrath of his masters. Abel was arrested on the basis of Hayhanen's evidence, and in October 1957 was sentenced to the electric chair. Appeals commuted this to 30 years in jail, and in February 1962, he was sent back to Russia in exchange for Francis Gary Powers, the U2 spy-plane pilot shot down over Sverdlovsk two years earlier.

A press officer for the World Health Organisation in Geneva defected to Britain in March, 1980. Ilya Grigorivich Dzhirkvelov was a KGB officer who had served three years in the Swiss city – a vital espionage nerve centre. After a carefully planned escape with his wife and seven-year-old daughter, he compromised scores of Soviet agents in Western Europe, especially in France and Belgium.

and the KGB took tighter control of GRU activities. Many agents were recalled or left without instructions for months while counter-espionage experts tried to assess the damage Penkovsky caused.

Nine years later, Soviet leader Leonid Brezhnev cut short a tour in Eastern Europe to attend a hasty meeting at Moscow airport with KGB spymaster Yuri Andropov and other top Communist party officials. As a result of their discussions, key spies were ordered home from Mexico, Canada, Finland, Greece, Germany, France, Nigeria and the Far East.

The cause of the Kremlin's consternation was the unprecedented mass expulsion of 105 Russian diplomats and trade officials by Britain on 24 September 1971. MI6 and the CIA were already aware that most of them were spies. But it was the defection of Oleg Adolfovitch Lyalin which revealed the full extent of their espionage activities. For Lyalin was an officer in the KGB's Department V, responsible for sabotage and assassination. And his evidence so enraged Prime Minister Edward Heath and Foreign Secretary Sir Alec Douglas Home that they warned Moscow that if any reprisals against Western envoys followed the exit orders, even more Soviets would be kicked out.

Lyalin arrived in London in 1969, with the cover of an official at the Soviet trade delegation based in Highgate. The security services soon discovered that, although he was a married man with a family in Russia, he was having an affair with his secretary. He also showed a liking for the luxuries of Western life, particularly drink. And in August 1971, two police officers stopped his car after seeing it being driven erratically. A blood-alcohol test proved positive. Lyalin had no diplomatic immunity. The consequences of a court case and return to Russia in disgrace were pointed out to him. In return for plastic surgery to protect him from possible assassination attempts, he agreed to cooperate with the authorities.

He revealed staggering details of what Attorney General Sir Peter Rawlinson later described in Parliment as 'the organization of sabotage within the United Kingdom and the elimination of individuals judged to be enemies of the USSR.'

Teams of saboteurs had been prepared to exact maximum damage on British radar stations, communications centres and other sensitive defence complexes in the 24 hours before any surprise attack by the Soviet Union. Lyalin's specific target was to blow up the Fylingdales early warning system in Yorkshire, on constant watch for missile attacks. He had maps showing where he was to link up with Russian commandos on the coast.

Lyalin also outlined plans for specially-adapted Aeroflot airliners to drop mines into the Clyde Estuary, trapping the nuclear submarine fleet at Holy Loch; for the London Underground system to be flooded; and for teams of already-recruited British traitors to attack British and American air bases, using arms and equipment from clandestine stores already established in the countryside. Since NATO contingency plans consider Britain an off-shore aircraft carrier for American reinforcements in the event of conventional warfare anywhere in Europe, the implications of a strong subversive army ready to strike at the defences from behind were horrific. Sadly for MI6 and the CIA, Lyalin knew few names of those involved. And he warned of a parallel network of GRU agents working separately from the KGB teams.

Britain made a formal protest to Soviet Foreign Minister Andrei Gromyko, circulated a full list of all the expelled Russians to friendly countries, and followed up Lyalin's leads as best it could at home and abroad. Specific details about the extent of Soviet preparations to attack other countries in peacetime were not released to the public, possibly for fear of causing too much alarm. But the counter-espionage forces of the West were left in no doubt that their task had taken on a sinister new dimension.

In the 1950s and early 1960s, most Iron Curtain defections were handled by the Americans. The CIA had a far bigger budget than MI5 or MI6, and could afford the time and money for the long, delicate task of 'turning' a Soviet agent. Also, many of the spies fleeing from the KGB or agencies of Russia's satellite countries insisted that the CIA keep Britain in the dark because both MI6 and MI5 had been infiltrated by Moscow moles. The 1945 Volkov debacle, detailed earlier, had taught subsequent defectors a lesson. Igor Gouzenko, Anatoli Golitsin, and Polish defector Michal Goleniewski were just three Communist renegades petrified of betrayal by a British spy chief. The 1971 defection of Oleg Lyalin in London was taken as evidence that MI6 and MI5 were now mole-free. And 11 years later the British landed an even bigger fish.

Vladimir Andreyevitch Kuzichkin was described by one intelligence source as the West's most precious catch for 30 years when he arrived in London with bulging dossiers of Soviet secrets in October 1982, and was taken to a Sussex hideaway for debriefing by British and American inquisitors. The Russian vice consul in the Iranian capital Tehran was really the KGB's spymaster in the Middle East, and brought with him a breakdown of the espionage network both there and in Western Europe, complete with code-names, code systems, the identities of agents and sub-agents, and details of KGB operations.

More inspired intelligence leaks were forthcoming about Kuzichkin than most defectors, possibly because the espionage organizations were still stung by the publicity battering they had taken over the Geoffrey Prime case, to be discussed later in this book. The West needed a morale booster – and Kuzichkin was it. Hints were dropped that he had worked as a double agent for Britain for up to five years, that he was lured by the love of a beautiful Egyptian-born MI6 girl working in Tehran, that his usefulness to Britain and America was on a par with Philby's value to Moscow at the height of his powers.

Kuzichkin's main task in Tehran was to infiltrate agents into the Iranian Communist party, the Tudeh, to foment subversion against the regime of Ayatollah Khomeini, which was proving less than pliable to the Kremlin's will. But he had access to sensitive KGB material affecting espionage throughout the Middle East and the NATO countries. Then, in June 1982, his British controllers learned he was about to be unmasked as a traitor. Unable to spirit him secretly out of Iran, they struck a deal with Khomeini's security police. Kuzichkin was delivered to them, and provided enough evidence for the arrest of Tudeh leader Hassein Zadeh and hundreds of his followers. Soviet influence inside Iran was effectively smashed. Then the defector was taken to Paris, and handed to the British. His wife elected not to follow him.

In accordance with diplomatic protocol, the Russian ambassador in London was allowed to request a meeting with Kuzichkin. But the spy who came in from the cold war was not interested. He knew that his information would force the KGB to completely reorganize their operations in at least ten countries. And for that, they were hardly likely to thank him.

Chapter Six

Sex Spies

Mata Hari is history's most legendary sex-and-secrets spy. Cynthia Payne took erotic espionage to new dimensions during World War 2. But even they might blush at the romantic ruthlessness of more recent amorous agents . . .

The Brothel Sneakers

Espionage has been called the second oldest profession in the world. And since Biblical times, spymasters have never been slow to use the services of the oldest to satisfy their own aims. The Book of Joshua tells how two Israelite agents, sent into Jericho in 1200 BC before an assault on the city, went straight to a house where the arrival of men raised no eyebrows – that of prostitute Rahab. Over the ages, all nations have paid alluring girls to tantalize targets and loosen tongues. But seldom have brothels been so cynically and clinically exploited for spying as in the last 45 years. And the Germans have led the way.

The sex-and-secrets trend was set by Nazi espionage genius Walter Schellenberg. In 1939 Gestapo chief Reinhard Heydrich ordered him to infiltrate reliable beauties into an exclusive bordello to pass on pillow talk. Worried by security leaks as war approached, Heydrich wanted to identify and eliminate blabber-mouths by tempting them with wine and women. But Schellenberg had his own ambitions for power. And he developed his boss's idea into an ingenious plan to gain a hold over his superiors. Instead of merely planting girls in Berlin's top house of ill repute, he decided to take it over completely. Fate had made that easy.

Madame Kitty Schmidt ran the classiest joint in town at 11 Giesebrecht-strasse. Though charges were high, the most distinguished and influential people in the country flocked to her rooms, assured of complete discretion and the attention of Germany's most lovely call girls. Kitty was coining it in. But Schellenberg knew what she was doing with her profits. Disturbed by Hitler's rise, and persecution of the gentle Jews among her clientele, she was secretly transferring takings to British banks and helping Jews escape Blackshirt harassment. When she too tried to leave Berlin on 28 June 1939, Gestapo agents were waiting at the German-Dutch border. Faced with a dossier of her 'crimes', and warned that she faced death or concentration camp incarceration, she had little choice but to agree to Schellenberg's sinister scheme.

Nazi workers moved into 11 Giesebrechtstrasse and gutted the interior. Ten third-floor rooms were wired with microphones, linked to a multi-core cable which ran to the cellar, where five monitoring desks were installed. Each had two recording turntables, enabling eavesdroppers to commit ten separate conversations to wax discs. Elsewhere in the city, vice squads carried out unusually frequent raids on nightclubs, dance bars and street corners. Hundreds of prostitutes were interrogated by SS men, psychiatrists and doctors. Finally a shortlist of 90 'emotionally reliable' girls was whittled down to 20 in seven days of non-stop tests. The chosen few were then given an intensive seven-week training course in foreign languages, military uniforms and decorations, and politics and economics at home and abroad. Radio interviewers taught them how to use innocent conversation to draw out secrets. Finally all was ready.

Madame Kitty was briefed on her new-style operations in March 1940. She was to carry on business as before, using old customers and existing girls. But every so often, clients would arrive using a code introduction: 'I come from Rothenburg.' These men were to be shown an album containing photographs of the 20 hand-picked beauties. When the special guest had made his choice, Kitty was to phone the girl. She would arrive within ten minutes, and leave immediately her mission was complete. Kitty was to do as she was told, and ask no questions about the 20 girls or their clients. And she had to sign an official secrets form which meant death if she breathed one word about what was happening.

Within days, the Rothenburg Romeos began to arrive. And as word spread on the cocktail party circuit, visiting dignitaries, army generals and staff from Berlin embassies began flocking to the pleasure palace. Soon the 20 girls were loving round the clock as special guests outnumbered genuine clients, and the

---

A top Soho vice king helped British spymasters establish two brothels in strife-hit Belfast in 1970. The houses of ill repute, set up in the Malone Road and Antrim Road areas, were designed to blackmail influential Ulstermen into providing information. Cameras hidden behind two-way mirrors captured them cavorting with hand-picked prostitutes from London and Dublin, who were paid £500 a week for their sexy spying. Knowledge of what the IRA and Protestant terror groups were up to improved dramatically. One compromized client gave the authorities the names and addresses of the killers of three British soldiers. But in 1972 the IRA discovered the truth about the brothels via a tapped telephone line. And on October 2, Provo gunmen attacked both the brothels and the Four Square Laundry, another intelligence-gathering fake business. Six British agents were said to have been killed, including one girl, but the Northern Ireland Office admitted only one casualty – a soldier driving a laundry van.

Gestapo had to send in extra food and drink to augment Kitty's rations. In one month, nearly 3,000 wax discs were recorded. By the end of 1940, more than 10,000 randy Rothenburgers had climbed the stairs to the luxurious love nests. All came away delighted by the nubile and knowledgeable girls. But Schellenberg wore the most satisfied smile.

One night, he overheard an astonishing tirade against Hitler by Italian Foreign Minister Count Galeazzo Ciano, who listed the German leader's shortcomings as statesman, soldier and lover. After the Führer read Schellenberg's transcript, relations between the two countries were never the same again. In September, the SS man eavesdropped as German Foreign Minister Joachim von Ribbentrop discussed a bizarre plan to occupy Gibraltar with his Spanish counterpart, Don Ramon Serrano Suner. Schellenberg was able to tip off SS chief Heinrich Himmler in time to quash it.

Operation Kitty continued for more than two years. The only time the bugging devices were turned off was during Reinhard Heydrich's increasingly frequent 'tours of inspection'. But as the war went badly for Germany, the love-and-listen network became a tool for settling old scores against rivals in the Nazi hierarchy. And, unknown to the Gestapo, the eavesdropping was no longer for their ears only. In December 1940, Lljubo Kolchev, a junior press secretary at the Rumanian embassy, had spotted workmen re-routing the multi-core cable through a drainpipe. And he suddenly realized what lay behind the Rothenburg stories he had heard on the diplomatic grapevine. For Kolchev was really Roger Wilson, a British spy. When he reported his findings to London, Allied spymasters quickly cashed in. Wilson became a frequent visitor to Madame Kitty's, keeping his eyes and ears open without arousing suspicion. And British communications experts tapped three wires in the cable.

In July 1942, an Allied bomber scattered Kitty's elegant furniture all over Giesebrechtstrasse. The Gestapo threw a ring of soldiers round the street while the secret wiring was transferred to the ground floor, left undamaged by the blast, but within a year the operation was terminated. Kitty was given complete control of the house again, and most of the 20 sexy spies agreed to stay with her. She kept her promise never to reveal Schellenberg's secret until her death, at 71, in 1954.

Schellenberg was arrested by the Allies in 1945, but by then his 25,000 incriminating wax discs had disappeared. They vanished from the Meinecke-strasse headquarters of the Gestapo as Russian troops entered rubble-strewn Berlin. And the only Westerner who claims to have seen them since is author Peter Norden. He wrote that, in 1963, they were stored in a secret vault in the offices of the East German security services. Doubtless inspired by their contents, the East Germans and their KGB masters have taken

Reinhard Heydrich

Schellenberg's brothel bugging to new heights of sophistication – sometimes with astonishing results.

In the early 1950s, Lydia Kuzazova set up an exclusive massage parlour near the centre of Frankfurt. Word soon spread that exotic and erotic girls were prepared to offer services beyond the call of duty behind Lydia's outwardly-respectable doors, and industrialists, diplomats, army officers and civil servants soon became regulars. But sex was not the only secret at the parlour. Unknown to the clients who let sensuous sensations get the better of commonsense, microphones recorded their words and hidden cameras filmed their love-making. The KGB soon built up a library of potential blackmail targets. But that was not the major reason for Lydia's tender trap.

Sixteen kilometres (10 miles) outside the city lay Camp David, the European operations centre of the CIA. Here agents were briefed for missions behind the Iron Curtain, and debriefed on their return. Lonely Americans far from home found comfort at Lydia's love palace. And one in particular paid a heavy price for his passion. Glen Rohrer, a 44-year-old sergeant at Camp David, operated the lie-detector equipment used in debriefing agents. He thus knew the names, cover identities, methods and targets of almost every spy who passed through the centre. Soon after he began visiting Lydia's lovelies in 1960, he was shown compromising film of himself, and warned that his superiors would see it unless he cooperated. For nearly five years, he gave the KGB all the names and addresses they needed. Hundreds of agents were arrested. Then, in August 1965, a KGB mole in West German counter-intelligence warned Lydia that Rohrer was under suspicion. While Rohrer drove to the Czech border to escape arrest, Lydia fled back to Moscow, leaving CIA chiefs to assess the consequences of the staggering betrayal.

The Russians got away with another successful sex-snooping operation in the exclusive Bonn suburb of Bad Godesberg between 1969 and 1972. And though Madame Marta's brothel was almost next door to the city's police headquarters, it was 1978 before the authorities were alerted to Marta by a defector. The slim young redhead was running a massage parlour near the West German capital when she was recruited to the KGB cause during a holiday in Moscow. She was promised funds to set up a more ambitious establishment if she turned a blind eye to eavesdropping.

A four-bedroomed apartment was wired for sound and picture sur-veillance, and Marta and her harem of beauties quickly attracted civil servants and diplomats from nearby government offices and embassies. Tapes and films were sent regularly to Moscow by the former gym teacher, and when she was finally arrested, West German counter-intelligence had to discover what the KGB had learned – and who they had blackmailed. But the Marta mystery was nothing to the puzzle they had to unravel 15 years earlier.

Hans Albert Heinrich Helmcke was perhaps the most extraordinary brothel sneaker of all time – because he sold secrets gleaned from between the sheets to both sides. A wartime gangster and black-marketeer, he emigrated to America in 1953, inherited more than £25,000 from two wealthy German-Americans he befriended, and in 1961 returned to Berlin, where he bought the Pension Clausewitz, once a brothel for both Nazi and Allied soliders, but later a legitimate hotel. Helmcke restored it to its wartime use, installing soft lights and deep leather furniture, and recruiting the pick of Berlin's ladies of the night. Soon he had established a lucrative trade, numbering politicians, law enforcement chiefs, film stars and sports personalities among his regular clients. But Helmcke was hungry for more money. When West German spy chiefs approached him to report on who frequented the brothel, and what they said, he rightly reasoned that the East Germans would like to have the same information.

For four years he kept his two masters happy, augmenting what he learned from his bugged bedrooms by setting up a detective agency and launching a news service for papers, both legitimate excuses for fact-finding. To cover his sale of secrets to an Iron Curtain country, he founded a canned meat business which existed only on paper. And he quickly earned enough to invest in nightclubs and hotels, Mercedes cars and a luxurious villa. The delighted East Germans even saved Helmcke the chore of recruiting girls. They sent some of their own specially-trained beauties to work for him.

But another of his employees sent the espionage empire crashing in 1965. The Pension Clausewitz manager, disgruntled when his expansion ideas were ignored, and upset when one of Helmcke's girlfriends started telling him how the brothel should be run, told the West Germans how their secrets were being shared. Police swooped on the pleasure palace, taking away

---

The West has rarely shared German and Russian enthusiasm for brothel espionage, though NATO spymasters have been forced to resort to the tactic. Just after World War 2 both the British and French security services paid German and Austrian prostitutes to sleep with Russian soldiers in the occupying forces. It was said that the French had 400 sexy agents 'doing their best on their backs in the Vienna Woods'. And in Paris, the French SDECE intelligence service combined with the CIA in an attempt to blackmail brothel guests from Eastern bloc nations, but without spectacular success.

microphones, recording equipment, tapes and a notebook listing East German telephone numbers. News of Helmcke's arrest rocked Berlin high society. Everyone anticipated a full-scale scandal. In the event, the sex-and-secrets double agent was jailed for only a few months. He later bragged: 'Berlin does not realize what it owes me – I could have blown society wide open.'

Helmcke, who was killed in 1973 when two minor thugs panicked during a kidnap attempt to extort money, had refined the brothel-espionage technique in unprecedented ways. But already another kind of sex spy was emerging ... an amorous agent even more ruthlessly ready to exploit sensual gratification ...

Swallows: From Russia With Love

Major James Holbrook turned away from the window of the small hotel room and gazed again at the beautiful girl stretched out on his bed. She made it hard for the American military attaché to concentrate on the task which had brought him from the embassy in Moscow to the small town of Rovno, a few miles east of the Soviet border with Poland. He was supposed to check rumours that Russia was preparing to invade its neighbouring satellite, plunged into turmoil in 1981 by Solidarity demands for economic and political reform. Then he had met the girl ...

He returned to her inviting arms. Holbrook, 41, had never met anyone so skilled at loving, so ready to pander to his every whim. Her embraces were a lonely man's only comfort in such a bleak outpost. But as they clung together again, the door was abruptly kicked down, camera flashbulbs exploded harshly, and a Russian colonel known to the American walked into the room. He gently pointed out that, as a married man with two children, Holbrook had seriously compromised himself. However, his Soviet friends could ensure that his wife and the embassy never heard of the incident if Holbrook cooperated by providing Moscow with a little information.

Holbrook was no naïve amateur in the espionage game. He courageously confessed his indiscretion to his superiors and was recalled to Washington. An intelligence spokesman there said:

'We can only guess that the Russians got wind of the fact that Major

Holbrook was being considered for a new job as military adviser to Vice President George Bush at the White House. He would have had access to the most highly secret material of President Reagan's administration.'

Holbrook had been hooked by a 'swallow', one of the hundreds of stunningly lovely Russian girls ruthlessly trained at specialist camps to cold-bloodedly seduce Westerners. And the fact that an agent well-versed in KGB espionage techniques could be tempted proved how effectively the beauties learn their lessons. But Moscow leaves nothing to chance in its efforts to recruit shamed victims of sex traps as spies. Targets are meticulously scrutinized for 'personality defects'. If a man has an eye for a pretty girl, the KGB provides one exactly suited to his tastes. And it has plenty of erotic experts to select from.

In his book *Sexpionage*, author David Lewis tells of an interview he had in Tunisia with Vera, a swallow who defected. She told him how the KGB recruited intelligent and attractive girls from schools and colleges with promises of salaries and privileges superior to those of most Russians in return for unspecified duties for the state. They were then taken to heavily guarded camps in remote areas for a de-humanizing course, designed to rid them of all inhibitions. First they watched films of every sexual activity, including perversions. Then they were ordered to strip in front of other women. Later men watched them undress, and caressed and criticised their bodies. Then coachloads of soldiers arrived, and the girls were ordered to make love to the complete strangers. Their performances were filmed for group discussion later. After several weeks, the girls lost all shame, and were ready to fall in with any suggestion for group or single sex.

As Vera told Lewis:

'We were told we should remember that we were soldiers fighting in

---

Indonesian President Achmed Sukarno had a worldwide reputation as a womaniser, so it was only natural that the KGB should try to blackmail him with a sex trap when he visited Moscow. He was introduced to a stream of expertly-trained beautiful swallows, and filmed making love to all of them in his hotel suite. But when the evidence was shown to him prior to a blackmail bid, Sukarno amazed the Soviet agents by asking for copies of the films to take home for public showing, adding: 'My people will be really proud of me.' The recruiting attempt went no further.

the front line of a bitter ideological battle. In war soldiers were often
ordered to do things which, as individuals, they would find
repulsive; but hard sacrifices were essential. Our bodies were
weapons to be used in a cause. By the time our training was
completed, we were hard, cynical, sophisticated young women
capable of bedding any heterosexual man authority selected for us,
and giving him the time of his life.'

Vera said she became sickened by her role as a sexy spy in 1963, after
seducing a young Frenchman about to get married. He was told his bride-to-
be would learn of the liaison unless his father, an influential chief in the
mining industry in France, passed over commercial secrets. The boy killed
himself by walking in front of a car in Moscow's Red Square, unable to cope
with the shame of his seemingly 'innocent affair'. Vera then seduced a senior
KGB official in return for official papers allowing her to visit East Berlin,
where she defected.

The French, with their traditional partiality for *amour*, have been special
targets for swallows. And it was the suicide of another sex trap victim,
Moscow air attaché Colonel Louis Guibaud, that prompted the defection in
London in 1963 of Yuri Krotkov, a film scriptwriter used by the KGB to set up
seductions, often using actresses as bait. What disillusioned Krotkov told MI 5
stunned his interrogators and rocked the French establishment. For he
revealed that France's ambassador to Russia had been compromised by at

---

Top politicians and diplomats are not the only victims of
Soviet swallow sex traps. Ordinary Western workers on
assignment behind the Iron Curtain can have their lives
disrupted by amorous agents. In July 1979, the 54-year-old
wife of British engineer Richard Clasper received a manila
envelope at her Tyneside home. It contained photographs of
her 57-year-old husband making love to a beautiful young
brunette. Mrs Clasper collapsed with shock and was rushed
to hospital. Her husband told reporters that, despite
warnings from Special Branch detectives before he left for
Russia, he succumbed to loneliness at the remote building
site where he was working, and went to bed with a 27-year-
old interpreter. A mysterious stranger then arrived, asking
him to spy on Russian workers at the site, but he refused.
Clasper added: 'It was the first time I had been unfaithful in
31 years. This has wrecked my marriage, broken my wife
and ruined me.'

least two swallows.

Maurice Dejean arrived in Moscow with his pretty young wife in 1955, and was quickly picked out by KGB sex trap mastermind Lieutenant General Oleg Gribanov as a likely target. His roving eye made him vulnerable. Krotkov, who had previously compromised Mexicans, Indians, Pakistanis, Americans and Britons, decided to win the ambassador's trust by charming his wife, Marie Claire. After engineering a meeting at a diplomatic reception, he cultivated the acquaintance by inviting her on river cruises, providing tickets to the ballet, and picking up the bill for lavish dinners. Eventually Dejean joined them on the social outings. Krotkov introduced him to a buxom, sophisticated interpreter called Lydia. Then, after arranging for Madame Dejean to enjoy a day away in the country, he invited the ambassador to an exhibition of paintings.

The lovely Lydia just happened to be admiring the pictures when they arrived. Within hours, she and Dejean were lovers.

Having photographed the event, the KGB already had a hold on the French envoy. But Lydia was known to be divorced. To spring their trap, the Russians needed another swallow. Lydia was sent out of Moscow 'to film on location' and Dejean was introduced to another actress, Larissa. Within days they too were bed partners. But in June 1958, the amorous ambassador received a nasty shock. Two burly men burst into Larissa's love nest. One played the part of an outraged husband. Dejean was left in no doubt that he would hear more about his adultery.

Worried, he consulted one of the friends Krotkov had introduced to him – Gribanov himself. He was reassuring, promising to try to pull strings. Within days, he was able to set the ambassador's mind at ease. The 'husband' had agreed not to press charges. But Dejean was now dangerously entangled. One day, the KGB would expect repayment for this 'favour'.

After Krotkov's defection, Dejean was recalled to Paris by his close friend, President De Gaulle, and grilled by counter-espionage men. It seemed the KGB had never called in the debt. De Gaulle dismissed him with the words, 'So Dejean, you enjoy the company of women.' It turned out he was not the only ambassador to share this hobby.

A blonde Russian swallow brought the distinguished diplomatic career of Sir Geoffrey Harrison to an abrupt end when she seduced him in Moscow. Sir Geoffrey was recalled to London in 1968, and it was thought at the time that the departure of Britain's ambassador was a protest at Russian intervention to crush liberalism in Czechoslovakia.

Only 13 years later was it revealed that he had had a torrid affair with a chambermaid called Galia at the embassy. When shown photographs of himself with her, and invited to become a Soviet spy, he wisely confessed to his Foreign Office bosses.

Sir Geoffrey said after a Sunday newspaper disclosed his secret:

'I did not ask Galia if she worked for the KGB, but the assumption was there. I regret it, of course I regret it. I was warned before I went to Moscow about this sort of thing – anyone going to the Iron Curtain countries is warned this can happen. It was a very silly thing for me to do.'

His replacement as ambassador to Moscow, Sir Duncan Wilson, said:

'Galia was a blonde, buxom girl and very attractive. There was no doubt she was one of the Russians' top drawer girls. She was clearly in a completely different class from the rest of the domestics, but I have no idea how good she was at housework – I dismissed her a few days after I arrived.'

Sir Duncan was astonished to receive a phone call days later from the Australian ambassador. 'It appeared Galia had gone straight round and asked him to give her a job, and he wanted to know if I could give her a reference,' he said. 'I made it quite clear she would not be at all suitable.'

How many Britons, Americans and West Europeans have been inveigled into espionage by the attentions of captivating Russian swallows? Commander Anthony Courtney, a former Naval Intelligence officer who later became a Conservative MP, has estimated the total of silent, shamed moles in the NATO countries at 10,000. And he says there are at least 50 in the British Foreign Office.

His opinions have particular relevance. For Commander Courtney was the first known victim of a sex trap used to discredit rather than recruit. In 1961, shortly after the death of his first wife, he was befriended on a business trip to Moscow by beautiful swallow Zina Volkova, who was working as an Intourist car rental assistant. Largely at her instigation, he took her back to his room in the National Hotel, and found comfort in her arms. Two years later, back in London, the Commander made a series of speeches in Parliament questioning the diplomatic immunity of employees at Soviet bloc embassies, and claiming that 20 chauffeurs at the Russian embassy in Kensington were KGB officers.

In August 1965, copies of intimate photographs of Courtney and Zina were delivered to influential MPs, the *News Of The World* newspaper and the Commander's second wife. Courtney was able to explain them to his wife and the security services, but the public were less reasonable. He lost his job as MP for Harrow East, and his political career was finished. Moscow does not usually take such drastic steps over critics on the back benches at Westminster, and many believe the public shaming of Courtney was a warning to somebody even better placed in the power structure, to toe the Kremlin line or else.

Anthony Courtney

Lonely Hearts and Ruthless Ravens

A flock of ravens proved in March, 1979, that beautiful female swallows are not the only agents to come from Russia with love. Ravens was the nickname given to handsome, smooth-talking Casanova comrades who moved into Western Europe's administrative capitals in force to seduce lonely secretaries. Once the love-hungry girls were hooked, NATO's most sensitive secrets were Moscow's for the taking. And they were taken in their hundreds. Only when four secretaries fled to East Germany in one week was the scope of the problem realized. Yet the espionage exploits of reds in the beds were no new phenomenon.

It was the summer of 1960 when Leonore Heinz cautiously opened the front door of her Bonn apartment. There stood Heinz Suetterlin, nervously fiddling with a bunch of red roses. He explained that he had been given the address after answering an advertisement in a newspaper 'lonely hearts' column, but now he could see there had been some terrible mistake. Leonore, 35 and frightened of being left on the marital shelf, was intrigued by the flattery, and invited the charming caller in for coffee. In fact there had been no mistake. Lonely Leonore was the carefully-selected target for a ruthless romantic assault.

Suetterlin had been meticulously coached for the task. He had learned how to live in the West at specially created camps in Russia. Whole towns, complete with shops, cinemas and restaurants, have been built there to simulate major cities in Britain, America, Germany and Japan. Spies live there for months, familiarizing themselves with their future enviroments by speaking only the language of their eventual destination, learning all about its currency and way of life.

As a raven, Suetterlin was then trained in every trick of seduction and making love. Nubile Soviet girls act as sex tutors during lessons which, according to one 1960s defector, are 'designed to turn us into animals capable of satisfying the cravings of any woman'. The defector said the pressure on the Red Romeos was so intense that two of his classmates committed suicide. But Suetterlin was made of sterner stuff.

Over coffee, he used every ounce of his practised charm on Leonore. She was amazed to find how much they had in common. They talked all evening, and made a date for dinner the next night. Concerts and romantic walks along the banks of the Rhine followed. Soon Leonore was hopelessly in love with Suetterlin. He was gentle, considerate and generous, in bed and out of it. Within six months they agreed to marry. Leonore was the envy of all her colleagues in the West German government's Foreign Ministry.

But the honeymoon was soon over. Weeks after their wedding, Suetterlin asked his bride to bring home classified documents from the office. Fear of losing the man she had waited for so long persuaded Leonore to do as he wished. She was given a handbag with a false compartment into which she put the papers just before going home to lunch. While she cooked their meal, Suetterlin photographed the secrets, which were returned to the Foreign Ministry during the afternoon. The Kremlin left instructions and picked up undeveloped rolls of film from hidden 'dead letter box' hiding places in derelict buildings or tree stumps. Suetterlin was alerted to each delivery when a tango titled 'Moscow Nights' was played on Radio Moscow.

In six years, more than 3,000 highly-classified documents found their way to KGB headquarters. They included full details of two vital NATO exercises to test the combat-readiness of West Germany's front-line forces, minutes of crucial NATO conferences and warnings of counter-intelligence operations against Iron Curtain espionage agents. Secret missile centres and evacuation plans in the event of a Russian invasion were also betrayed to Moscow. And the Suetterlin-Leonore service was so efficient that KGB chiefs began to suspect it. Surely, they reasoned, no security service could be lax enough to allow leaks on this scale. But it was.

The Suetterlin operation came to an end in 1967 only because Yevgeny

---

Moscow also trains good-looking men as homosexual ravens. One was involved in the blackmail trap which recruited British Admiralty spy William Vassall in 1954. And three Soviet defectors told the West in the early 1960s that two other gay ravens compromised John Watkins when he was Canadian Ambassador to Russia. Hidden cameras had taken pictures, and Watkins was told they would be used to wreck his career unless he encouraged a pro-Soviet line in Canadian foreign policy. Watkins, at that time being considered for a Foreign Ministry job in Canada, was later ambassador to Denmark before retiring through ill health. He was recalled to Montreal for questioning after the defectors revealed his secret shame, but died from a heart attack, aged 62, after interrogation in October, 1964.

Runge, his spymaster, defected to the West, giving full details of that and other espionage coups. He told West German interrogators:

'The Suetterlins copied the personal files of diplomats and functionaries of the foreign service. These provided an ideal starting point for further entrapments or blackmail. Thanks to Lola [Leonore's KGB code name] we knew well ahead of time whenever an investigation had been ordered against any of our agents. We received copies of all Foreign Ministry messages which had to pass across Lola's desk on their way to the coding room. Often we read them in Moscow before the German Foreign Minister got a chance to read them in Bonn!'

The couple were arrested, but at first Leonore refused to say anything to incriminate her husband. Then she was shown his statement. She was only one of three women he had been sent to Germany to woo. He never loved or even liked her. Their meeting, courtship and marriage was all ordered by Moscow. During sex, his passion was always merely duty. Leonore said nothing as she read the harsh words. But that night she hanged herself in her cell with the cord from her dressing gown. Suetterlin was jailed for seven years.

Leonore Heinz was a tragic victim of the Bonn syndrome exploited so ruthlessly by Moscow. The artificially-created nerve centre of the West German and NATO administrations sucks in tens of thousands of ambitious girls as secretaries, receptionists, clerical assistants and switchboard operators. They have lavish apartments, responsible jobs, stylish cars and plenty of money. Only one thing is lacking – men. The bureaucrats they work with are mostly married and available only for short-term casual affairs. The nightlife is nowhere near as sophisticated as that of Paris, London or New York. The frustrated spinsters are vulnerable to any man who offers availability and diversion. And in the late 1970s there were suddenly scores of such men.

Helga Berger was 38, a secretary in the Foreign Ministry where Leonore had worked, when a stranger approached as she sat at a café beside the Rhine. Peter Krause, fortyish and well-dressed, soon swept her off her feet with expensive dinners, and nights at the opera, cinema and theatre. They became lovers and went on holiday together in Spain. Then came the catch. Krause said he worked for British intelligence, and introduced her to a man claiming to be the head of the UK secret service. There seemed no harm in obtaining classified papers for the agent of a NATO ally. Months later, Krause revealed the truth – he was an East German spy. By then, it was too late for Helga. For years she continued to provide him with information. 'I did not want to lose him,' she tearfully said at her trial. 'I loved him, loved him.' When she began a five-year jail sentence, Krause was back in East Germany.

SEX SPIES

Dagmar Scheffler was also left to pick up the pieces after being loved and deserted. Dagmar, 35, who worked in the personal office of the West German Chancellor, had just been divorced when smooth-talking Herbert Schroeter walked into her life. Soon she was providing him with details of West Germany's defence policy, the West's position on Soviet neglect of human rights and Bonn's attitude towards Moscow. Schroeter was warned in time to flee to Russia just before Dagmar was arrested. 'I needed a man and Herbert was my dream,' she said. 'I was besotted.'

Renate Lutze, 39, was another secretary duped by a raven. She passed more than 1,000 sensitive documents from her office – that of a top West German defence official – to the man who wooed and wed her during a six year espionage spree before they both were arrested.

Then, in March 1979, came the devastating defection of at least six secretaries in one month. Four fled across the Berlin Wall in one week. The six included Christel Broszey, 32-year-old chief secretary to the leader of the West German opposition, Inge Goliath, 35, secretary to the party's foreign affairs spokesman, Ingeborg Schultz, 36, from the Science Ministry, and Helga Roedinger, 44, who worked in the Finance Ministry.

A NATO spokesman said 'With every girl who has defected, we have found there was a Communist agent lover. When a girl has fallen for him, it is almost impossible for her to escape. She has found an attentive lover who is superb in bed because he has been trained to be.' West German counter-intelligence chief Herbert Hellenbroich said:

'These are older women who have achieved a position of trust and reliability by devoting themselves to their careers, then found they have nothing in their personal lives. They can easily be led into love, and Communist agents can even reveal their identity without the risk of being exposed. The woman will be dependent on them for love, terrified of losing the man who has brought romance into her life.'

But the raven problem was not unique to Germany. In the same month, March 1979, Ursel Lorenzen, secretary at NATO headquarters in Brussels to the man who planned all NATO military exercises, fled with her lover to East Berlin, and appeared on TV to accuse the West of having contingency plans which would reduce much of Central Europe – on both sides of the Iron Curtain – to a nuclear wasteland. Ursel, 38, took with her dossiers from NATO files, and security chiefs in Belgium described her betrayal as 'a devastating blow'.

Western spycatchers stepped up surveillance of possible ravens. They flooded the press with stories of how Communist agents signed on innocently at language schools and seduced girls studying to increase their qualifications for service in multi-national organizations. They put up posters in all NATO and government offices warning: 'There is a code word which opens safes – it is LOVE.' And for a while, the precautions seemed to work. Then, in April 1980, Belgian secretary Imelda Verrept failed to return to her job at NATO headquarters in Brussels after the Easter break. Imelda was in her thirties. She had an attentive new boyfriend. And she had gone away for the holiday with him ... to East Berlin. Shapex, a major military exercise to be held within weeks by NATO armies, was no longer a mystery to Moscow. Yet another raven had flown after cultivating a cuckoo in the West's nest.

But Russia's most sensational success in exploiting sex for espionage ends was not due to the work of randy ravens, sensuous swallows or manipulating madames. The Kremlin simply cashed in ruthlessly when a man who should have known better took a fancy to a girl he met purely by chance ...

The Spy Scandal that Ruined Profumo

Intrigued by shrieks of laughter from his stately home's swimming pool, Lord Astor guided his weekend guests towards the gate in the pool fence. They pushed it open just as a dazzling beauty emerged, naked from the water. She brushed her long, flowing dark red hair from her eyes – and then noticed the arrival of strangers. Their smiles broadened as she screamed for her swimming costume, and her companions threw it further from her. But the events of the next two years were to wipe those smiles from the faces of almost everyone present. The innocent fun of that summer afternoon in 1961 was to result in the disgrace of a British Government minister, the electoral defeat of his party after 13 years in power, the death of one of those present, serious doubts about a top spymaster, and praise and promotion for a Soviet agent. For the poolside frolic was the opening scene in the British political scandal of the century – the Profumo affair. And it is now clear that what Prime Minister Harold Macmillan at first described as 'a silly scrape over a woman' was, in fact, a carefully orchestrated Russian subversion triumph.

The beauty in the pool was Christine Keeler, then 20. She was staying at a cottage on Lord Astor's Cliveden estate with Dr Stephen Ward, an osteopath whose 'healing hands' had eased the pains of some of the richest and most powerful figures in British society. Lord Astor, grateful for past services, had given him use of the cottage in 1950. Now that generous gesture was to rebound on him savagely. For among his own party of weekend guests was War Minister John Profumo. And he was captivated by the lithe body so temptingly on display before him. Within days he had asked Ward to arrange a rendezvous with Christine. Soon she and the politician were lovers.

Such secret liaisons are not unusual among married members of Parliament. Labour security spokesman George Wigg, who played a leading role in the subsequent scandal, said: 'Few in the House of Commons have not been guilty of some sexual turpitude.' What caused Profumo's downfall was the identity of Ward's other companion that weekend at Cliveden. He was Captain Eugene Ivanov, a GRU master spy masquerading as assistant naval attaché at the Russian embassy in London.

Ward had been introduced to him by Sir Colin Coote, who was editor of the upmarket *The Daily Telegraph* newspaper. The osteopath treated him for lumbago, and happened to mention that, as a keen artist, he was anxious to go sketching in Moscow, but was having problems obtaining a visa. When Ivanov toured the *Telegraph*'s Fleet Street offices with a party of military attachés, Sir Colin remembered the conversation, and arranged a dinner for the two to meet. They quickly became friends. But unknown to the editor, neither man was what he seemed. And that was to prove catastrophic for Profumo.

One of Ward's sidelines was meeting young girls on the London nightclub circuit, and grooming them into high class prostitutes. Christine Keeler was a nude dancer at the Murray Cabaret Club when she fell under his hypnotic spell. Ward provided girls for visiting international dignitaries as well as his influential patients, and MI5 checked him out since he was moving in powerful circles. They were prepared to turn a blind eye to some of his less savoury antics in return for occasional information. And when he told of his acquaintance with Ivanov, MI5 chief Sir Roger Hollis hatched a bizarre plot to try to persuade the Soviet to defect. Ivanov was a known spy – double agent Oleg Penkovsky named him during debriefings by British and American interrogators – and Ward was ordered to ply him with Western luxuries, cultivating his passion for drink and women. Christine Keeler was one of those who shared his bed.

Sadly for MI5, Ivanov was a committed Communist who soon saw through the attempted entrapment. Ward, who had some socialist sympathies, may even have told him of it. The Russian reported the situation to Moscow while playing along with Hollis's scheme. He discovered that, in addition to providing girls for important people, Ward also took pictures of them making love through two-way mirrors. Ivanov obtained copies from three albums of incriminating photographs collected by the osteopath, and sent them to his masters for possible blackmail attempts. And when he found that Keeler was Profumo's mistress, he hinted that, if she coaxed from the minister the date on which America planned to equip West Germany's air force with nuclear weapons, Ward would have no more trouble getting his visa for Moscow.

There is no evidence that Keeler ever asked the question, and no suggestion that Profumo would have answered if she had. But news of what was in Ivanov's mind forced Sir Roger Hollis to act. Puzzlingly, he did not go to the War Minister himself, or the Prime Minister, or the Home Secretary, to whom he was directly responsible. Instead he told Cabinet Secretary Sir Norman Brook of Profumo's invidious position – then, astonishingly, asked Sir Norman if he would try to persuade Profumo to help in inducing Ivanov to defect. It was a ploy fraught with danger. No minister could be seen dabbling in espionage, let alone caught trying to subvert a foreign national, and Profumo had the good sense to reject the idea out of hand. At the same time, he decided to end his affair with Keeler, but unwisely did so by letter, using the word Darling. It was to be another nail in his political coffin . . . and in any case, it was too late for Profumo to wriggle out of his predicament.

The Opposition Labour Party was already sniping at the Tory Government over a series of spy scandals – the Portland ring, Admiralty spy William Vassall and double agent George Blake. George Wigg was spearheading the attack. On 11 November 1962, he received a mysterious phone call at the home of his political agent in Dudley. A muffled voice said: 'Forget Vassall, you want to look at Profumo.' Wigg and Profumo were not on the best of terms. They had clashed angrily in the Commons days earlier over the lack of heat acclimatization given to British troops before duty in the Middle East. But the call had not come from a political aide. In fact, Wigg, who died in August 1983, never found out who made it. It could have been a journalist anxious to bring unprintable rumour into the public spotlight. Equally, it could have been a mischief maker with a grudge against the War Minister. But security experts believe the call came from a Russian agent, intent on causing a scandal. If that was the Kremlin's aim, they were not kept waiting long.

Wigg and his aides began checking on Profumo. Christine Keeler confirmed she had been mistress of both the minister and Ivanov. And it was on the security danger rather than the moral issue of adultery that Wigg launched his assault with a Commons question on 21 March 1963. Labour Party chiefs and the whole of Fleet Street knew a scandal was inevitable. But Home Secretary Henry Brooke, to whom the Wigg question was addressed, was completely in the dark. Profumo foolishly denied any affair with Keeler. Then Brooke summoned Sir Roger Hollis, and demanded to know what was

Left:
Christine
Keeler

Below: John
and Valerie
Profumo

going on. The MI5 chief at last revealed what he had learned 18 months earlier – that Ivanov had asked Ward to get him the date of nuclear arms being given to Germany – but maintained that any security fears ended when Ivanov fled back to Moscow in January 1963, tipped off about the impending storm.

The Government, ill-informed by its top spymaster, now had its back to the wall. Christine Keeler had become involved with two West Indian lovers, one of whom was arrested for beating up the other and jealously firing shots at the home of Stephen Ward. Keeler, hard up for money, approached Fleet Street papers, offering to sell her story. She handed over Profumo's letter. Then she too fled the growing pressure. There were ugly rumours that the Establishment had got rid of her. She was traced to Madrid, still ready to tell her side of events for cash. Profumo continued to deny the affair. He lied to the House of Commons in a statement, and successfully sued an Italian magazine for libel when it doubted his word. But this was not a political squall that would blow over. Profumo went off to Venice on holiday with his wife, former actress Valerie Hobson. He decided to clear his conscience with her. They returned immediately to London where, on 4 June, he resigned as War Minister and as an MP – a job he had held for 25 years. His disgrace for contempt of the Commons was complete when his name was removed from the Privy Council.

The scandal was now at full flood, fuelled by the revelations of Christine Keeler, who sold her memoirs to a sensational Sunday newspaper for £23,000, and the sensational death of Stephen Ward. He took a drugs overdose in July while on bail facing charges of living on immoral earnings. He was described at his trial as a 'thoroughly filthy fellow' and 'a wicked, wicked creature'. But Sir Colin Coote, the man who made the ill-fated introduction to Ivanov, said: 'I should doubt whether a more trivial person has ever seriously embarrassed a government.' In fact, it became increasingly clear that both Ward and Keeler had merely been pawns in the game.

The House of Commons held a full debate on the Profumo affair on 17 June. Prime Minister Harold Macmillan was mercilessly mauled. He was forced to admit that no one had told him what was happening until it was too late to change the course of events. It was a staggering confession from the head of a government, and even arch antagonist George Wigg was embarrassed as he watched his political foe reeling from the twin blows of betrayed loyalty to a colleague and an appalling lack of information. Macmillan resigned as Conservative leader within 12 months, and many believe the Profumo debacle was a significant factor in the 1964 General Election defeat of his successor, Sir Alec Douglas Home, by Harold Wilson and the Labour Party.

MI5 chief Sir Roger Hollis watched Macmillan stumble through his Commons ordeal from the public gallery. He too was to retire within a year, possibly under pressure from members of Macmillan's Cabinet who felt he was grossly at fault for keeping them in the dark about Profumo's predicament and the fact that Ivanov had proved to be a spy worthy of expulsion. Later it was learned that Sir Roger had specifically forbidden full investigation of Ivanov's activities by MI5.

Sir Roger died in October 1973. Eight years later, writer Chapman Pincher analysed his career in the book *Their Trade Is Treachery*. He said the spymaster had done as little as possible as late as possible in the Profumo affair. He also accused him of doctoring a report of his interview with 1945 defector Igor Gouzenko; inexplicably suspending interrogation of Anthony Blunt for two weeks in 1964, thus giving the traitor time to consult his masters or destroy evidence; refusing to pursue inquiries against some of the men named as spies by Blunt; and presiding over MI5 at a time of conspicuous lack of success, partly because all anti-Communist operations were leaked to the targets. Pincher then pointed out that for more than a decade, Soviet

---

Moscow regards the United Nations skyscraper in New York as 'the tallest observation tower in the Western world for intelligence activity'. And half the 800 Soviets working in New York are espionage agents. That was part of the eye-opening evidence provided by Arkady Shevchenko when he sought asylum in America in April, 1978. Shevchenko, 48, a brilliant career diplomat and protégé of Foreign Minister Andrei Gromyko, had ambassador ranking at the UN, and was the highest-placed Russian ever to defect to the West. He did so, he said, because though Moscow talked about disarmament it was secretly involved in massive re-armament. A month after his defection – which followed two years as a covert CIA agent – his wife died from a mysterious overdose in Moscow. Then an Alabama call girl called Judy Chavez dragged Shevchenko into the headlines by revealing that, in a six month sex spree, he spent nearly $100,000 of CIA money towards a new sports car. They also shared a 10-day Caribbean holiday at the taxpayers' expense. Shevchenko survived the storm like a good diplomat, married another American girl, and settled quietly in Washington as a £17,000-a-year CIA consultant.

When counter-espionage agents finally caught up with sexy spy Karl Helfmann, he said 'Thank God, now I am safe from those women.' For Helfmann, nicknamed the Red Cassanova, was the most extraordinary Russian raven so far captured. He was nearly 60, and running a struggling wine business, when he was recruited at a trade fair in Leipzig in 1953. Iron Curtain countries agreed to buy his wine if he also provided secrets. So began a five-year love-in for the charming, sophisticated travelling salesman. He wooed secretaries in every town he visited, often bedding at least eight women a week as he went from Hanover to Frankfurt, from Düsseldorf to Bonn in his battered Volkswagen. His Communist controllers installed a hidden two-way radio in the car so they could contact him on his long drives. He seduced sources in West German government departments, scientific research laboratories, aircraft factories, steel plants and embassies, and received more than £15,000 for his efforts from his delighted – and amazed – spymasters. But in 1958 he was betrayed, possibly by a lover who saw him with one of her rivals. He was sentenced to five years hard labour. Compared to the previous five years, that was like a rest cure for Helfmann.

defectors were terrified of coming to Britain because they knew of a Russian mole in a powerful position. And he made the devastating claim that Sir Roger, a trusted agent for 25 years, was that mole.

Prime minister Margaret Thatcher denied the allegation in the House of Commons in 1981. And Sir Roger was also cleared of blame in Lord Denning's Committee of Inquiry report into the Profumo affair, issued in 1964. Perhaps he had given plausible explanations for the actions which so angered the Cabinet. Perhaps his role was minimized to avoid publicizing MI5, which is still officially non-existent. But there was an implied reproach for an unwise attempt to induce a defection in these words from Lord Denning:

'Captain Ivanov filled a new role in Russian technique. It was to divide the United Kingdom from the United States by devious means. If ministers or prominent people can be placed in compromising positions, or made the subject of damaging rumour, or the security service can be made to appear incompetent, it may weaken the confidence of the United States in our integrity and reliability ... If this was the object of Captain Ivanov, with Ward as his tool, he succeeded only too well.'

The meaning was clear. Hollis had continued to play with fire when he should have known better.

The Russians had not created the Profumo scandal, but they had manipulated it to full advantage. More evidence of their wiles emerged in America. A KGB officer working at the United Nations was providing the FBI with information which spymaster J. Edgar Hoover valued highly. In 1963 he told the FBI of a talk in Moscow with Ivanov, who claimed he had bugged Christine Keeler's bedroom, and gained valuable intelligence from her pillow talk with Profumo. Hoover sent the information to President Kennedy, but he declined to forward it to London, telling aides: 'Mr Macmillan is in enough trouble already.' In the event, the UN double agent was proved to be a stooge, feeding mischievous misinformation.

The fact that his career had been destroyed by a cynical Soviet scheme was no consolation for John Profumo, who withdrew from the spotlight with as much dignity as he could muster, and devoted his life to unpublicized charity work. He was ruined by his sexual appetite just as surely as those politicians and diplomats trapped by swallows and ravens. But at least he survived after getting caught up in the shadowy world of espionage. As we shall see in the next chapter, many others have not been so fortunate.

Chapter
Seven

Deadly Spies

Few real agents have the fictional licence to kill of
Ian Fleming's creation, James Bond. But
espionage can still be a deadly business – and not
just for the professionals ...

Bogdan Stashinsky: Hit-man with a Conscience

Bogdan Stashinsky lurked in the shadows outside the Munich apartment block and glanced again at his watch. It was almost 13.00. Then the car swung into the parking area. The man was alone. As he walked to the apartment door, fumbled for his key and started to turn the lock, Stashinsky slid silently forward, a slim metal tube 50 cm (19 in) long and 3 cm ($1\frac{1}{4}$ in) wide clutched in his right hand. He pressed a trigger and a glass ampoule exploded in the man's face. The victim staggered back as a spray of prussic acid sent lethal fumes into his body, contracting his blood vessels violently. By 13.05 he was dead. And Bogdan Stashinsky, on his way back to a hero's welcome in Moscow, reflected ruefully on the few precious moments that might have spared Ukrainian exile Stefan Bandera his life.

Stashinsky, handsome, clean-cut and 27 years old, was a KGB hit-man. A Ukrainian fluent in German thanks to the Nazi occupation of his homeland, he was recruited by Russia's secret service at 19, when caught on a train without a ticket. In 1957 he had carried out a similar assassination, also in Munich. Lev Rebet, another Ukrainian anti-Communist, died easily on the stairs to his office. An autopsy blamed a heart attack. Stashinsky survived the toxic fumes because of antidote pills. Now, on 15 October 1959, he had killed again. A month later in Moscow, KGB chairman Aleksandr Nikolaevich Shelepin presented him with the Order of the Red Banner for success in executing 'an important government commission'. There were hints, too, of further assassination assignments. Shelepin said he was to learn English to help in future 'difficult but honourable' work.

In fact, Stashinsky already knew he was incapable of any more cold-blooded killings. Even his first attempt to murder Bandera had failed because of his conscience. When he saw the target standing alone in a garage in May 1959, he turned and ran, throwing his poison tubes into a river. He told his controllers at a Karlshorst rendezvous that a stranger arrived just as he was about to strike, and the attempt had to be abandoned. Stashinsky hoped the KGB would call off the contract. The spy chiefs were adamant. Bandera must die. Five months later, as Stashinsky stood in the shadows of the apartment block, he made up his mind that he would abort the murder attempt if Bandera did not arrive by 13.00. Tragically, he drove up two minutes too soon.

Stashinsky re-lived his torment when he watched newsreel film of Bandera's funeral at a cinema. The grief of his wife and children affected the killer deeply. He shared his guilt with Inge Pohl, a girl he had fallen for after their meeting at Karlshorst. The KGB wanted him to abandon her and marry a fellow agent to help in future missions. Inge was a secret anti-Communist, but the lovers decided to conceal this in an attempt to stay together. She pretended to be ready to work for the KGB, and their marriage was finally given the go-ahead. But when Inge became pregnant, the spymasters considered the child a hindrance and put pressure on her to have an abortion or surrender the baby to the care of the state. The couple resolutely refused, and began to plot a way to defect.

Inge went to stay with her parents in Berlin, and gave birth to a boy there in March 1961. But Stashinsky was refused permission to visit her. Then, in August, Inge telephoned with terrible news. Their son had died from pneumonia. Stashinsky was allowed to fly to Berlin for the funeral – but only with a KGB escort. It was suggested to him that the death might be a ploy by the CIA to trap him and smuggle him to the West. Stashinsky was repelled that anyone could think like that. KGB surveillance was oppressive in the city, and the couple realized they had only one hope – escaping before the funeral service.

On the afternoon of 12 August – 24 hours before the Berlin Wall would seal the city for ever – they crawled from Inge's parents' home and scurried, crouching behind a hedge, to a side street out of sight of the KGB watchers. A taxi took them to the elevated railway to West Berlin, and Stashinsky went straight to the police at Tempelhof, and admitted who he was and what he had done. At first neither the Germans nor the Americans believed his astonishing story. But as they checked out his evidence, the pieces of the jigsaw mystery left by the deaths of Rebet and Bandera began to fall into place. And in October 1962, Stashinsky went on trial in public at Karlsruhe. He had been in the almost unique position of having to convince the authorities of his guilt, and in court he explained that he wanted to unburden his conscience 'and give worldwide publicity to the way in which "peaceful co-existence" really works in practice'.

After psychiatrists testified that the professional assassin was mentally healthy, the presiding judge, who had consulted the victims' families, caused a sensation by sentencing Stashinsky to only eight years jail, as an *accomplice* to murder. He said the defendant, 'gentle and peace-loving by nature', might have been a schoolteacher 'had it not been for the Soviet system which regards political murder on behalf of the state as a necessity'. And the judge went on: 'The guilt of those from whom he received his orders is far greater. The Soviet secret service no longer commits murder at its own discretion.

Murder is now carried out on express government orders. Political murder has, so to speak, become institutionalized.'

Kremlin leaders were aghast that the world now knew people were being killed in peacetime on direct orders from the Politburo. They had tried to clean up their image after the wholesale slaughter of Stalin's purges at home and abroad, and insisted that political killings be carried out only on written directives from the Central Committee of the Communist Party. Now that policy had rebounded on them.

Defectors told the West that the Stashinsky trial was followed by a big shake-up in both the KGB and Party leaderships. At least 17 officers were demoted or fired. But it was soon clear that Nikita Khruschev and Politburo chiefs did not regret the killings, only the fact that they had been unmasked as cynical plotters. Assassination programmes were cut back, but not forbidden. Orders went out that, in future, assassins would be hired foreign criminals or agents with no direct connection with the Soviet Union. And scientists at two secret laboratories at Kuchino, just outside Moscow, were instructed to step up their efforts to discover even more ingenious undetectable ways to make murder look like natural death ...

The Fatal Umbrella

Fear shot through the heart of Georgi Sergeevich Okolovich when he opened the door of his Frankfurt home on 18 February 1954, and he was confronted by a burly Russian. Okolovich, a leader of the prominent anti-Communist Soviet émigré group NTS, had survived two earlier kidnap attempts. Now it seemed Moscow had decided on more drastic action. The visitor, who introduced himself as Nikolai Chochlov, had written orders from the Communist Party Central Committee for Okolovich's execution. But after showing his victim the death warrant, Chochlov asked him to ring the West German authorities. And what he later told them was soon front page news around the world.

Chochlov, a secret service veteran, had sent dozens of men into free Europe to kill or kidnap influential critics of the Kremlin or refugees from the Russian regime. But when he himself was ordered to carry out a 'wet affair' – spy jargon for liquidating an enemy of the state – he knew it was his chance to escape. American and German counter-intelligence men arrested his two accomplices. Then Chochlov led them into woods outside Munich. There, hidden inside a car battery, was what seemed like a gold cigarette case. Chochlov demonstrated its real use – as an electric pistol which noiselessly fired dum-dum bullets coated in potassium cyanide.

At first the KGB merely tried to discredit their former agent. Moscow announced that his story was a CIA invention, that he and Okolovich were relatives and both Nazi war criminals. When Chochlov continued to speak out, more lethal steps were taken. In September 1957, he collapsed at a Frankfurt meeting with violent stomach pains and nausea. Within days of entering hospital, he was covered in hideous dark brown stripes and blotches, and black and blue swellings. Blood seeped through pores of his dry, shrunken skin. His hair fell out by the handful.

Suspecting poisoning by the toxic metal thallium, German doctors tried every known antidote without success. As the victim's bones decayed and his blood turned to plasma, Okolovich was told there was no hope for the man who had spared his life. But the reprieved Russian exile refused to give up. He persuaded a local American hospital to take over the case. Six top military surgeons began round-the-clock treatment at a heavily-guarded US Army camp. For a week massive injections of cortisone, vitamins, steroids and experimental drugs, plus continuous blood transfusions, kept the patient alive. Then, slowly, almost miraculously, he began to recover. By late October, totally bald and badly scarred, he was off the danger list.

Toxicologists later discovered exactly why Chochlov's complaint had been so difficult to cure. He had been poisoned with thallium exposed to intense atomic radiation, which made the metal disintegrate almost instantly through the system, destroying the white corpuscles of the blood and draining the body's life-sustaining fluids. Chochlov had been more than lucky to survive. Later victims of Eastern bloc poison attacks were not so fortunate.

On the evening of 7 September 1978, Georgi Markov was waiting for a bus on London's Waterloo Bridge after finishing work at the BBC World Service building nearby. Suddenly he felt a sharp pain in his thigh. Turning, he saw a man picking up an umbrella he had apparently dropped. The man mumbled an apology before leaping into a taxi. Markov went home for a quiet dinner with his wife. At bedtime, he began to feel unwell, and mentioned the umbrella incident to her for the first time. By 02.00 his temperature had reached 104° and an ambulance rushed him to hospital. He died there four days later.

At first the mysterious fever and nausea baffled doctors. Then an inch-by-inch search of the body using a magnifying glass revealed a tiny metal ball, measuring just 1.52 millimetres in diameter. The ball, made of a platinum and iridium mixture used in jet engines, had been expertly drilled with two microscopic connecting holes 0.35 mm wide. And they had been filled with ricin, a by-product of the process of extracting oil from the castor oil plant, and twice as deadly as cobra venom. There was then no known antidote.

Detectives found it impossible to trace the taxi driver, or witnesses from the bus queue. But painstakingly they built up a picture of what had happened. And the Battersea inquest was sufficiently convinced to record a verdict of unlawful killing.

Georgi Markov was a Bulgarian-born author and playwright who fled his homeland in June 1969, after a satirical stage performance he wrote upset the authorities. He became a broadcaster in the West, never afraid to speak his mind in radio transmissions to the Eastern bloc from both Britain and West Germany. 'He hated the regime,' his widow told the inquest. Increasingly, the regime of Bulgaria, the most Stalinist Soviet satellite country, hated his attacks. And in August 1978, a hit-man travelled to Western Europe with a double mission. In Paris he fired a pellet into the back of Bulgarian radio and TV reporter Vladimir Kostov during a Metro journey. Kostov was lucky – not enough of the poison, manufactured mainly in Czechoslovakia and Hungary – had been used and he survived after an agonizing battle in hospital.

Two weeks later there were no mistakes on Waterloo Bridge. Nobody noticed the pellet hit Markov, fired, it is believed, by a surgical implantation gun concealed in the umbrella tip. And had the victim not gasped, 'I have been poisoned, murdered,' as the lethal ricin more than doubled his white blood-cell count, the West might never have learned of yet another sinister Soviet bloc murder method.

Scotland Yard officers believed the assassination was organized independently by Bulgarian espionage agents, and Whitehall sources claimed the Russians were furious at the bad publicity it caused. But Western spycatchers remembered the Politburo orders following the Stashinsky defection, and began re-evaluating other sudden 'natural deaths'. One in particular has always concerned security chiefs.

On 18 January 1963, Hugh Gaitskell, moderate leader of the British Labour Party, died in hospital of systemic lupus erythematosus, a failure of the heart and kidneys. It was a complaint hardly ever seen in men over 40 in temperate climates, yet Gaitskell, 56, had contracted it less than a month after being released from hospital after treatment for viral pneumonia. Then Soviet defector Anatoli Golitsin told interrogators that, before he fled, the chief of the KGB's northern Europe section mentioned plans to kill an opposition party leader. And MI5 investigators discovered that, shortly before his death, Gaitskell had visited the Russian embassy in London to

Mr and Mrs Gaitskell

collect a visa for a trip to Moscow, and had been given coffee and biscuits.

Experts at Britain's Microbiological Research Establishment at Porton Down, Wiltshire, could not say how the disease might be caused – but CIA spymaster James Angleton discovered Soviet medical papers announcing success in experiments with a drug that could induce fatal heart and kidney failure. Though Gaitskell's widow and most of his Labour Party colleagues continued to believe the death was natural, top espionage men, including MI 5 chief Sir Martin Furnival Jones, kept an open mind. Gaitskell had fought hard to stop the Party swinging to the Left. Under his successors, extremist Marxists openly flaunted their views under Labour's banner.

Hermann Luedke: NATO's Traitorous Rear Admiral

Americans accustomed to casting Soviet spies as the bad guys in a worldwide espionage war were given a shock in 1975 when three US government investigations revealed that the CIA had used assassination as a weapon in diplomacy. Witnesses swore on oath that the killings of Congo chief Patrice Lumumba, Dominican Republic leader Rafael Trujillo and South Vietnam's Ngo Dinh Diem were all sponsored by the American intelligence agency. And espionage sources told newsmen that a CIA hit-team was in Beirut hunting Kim Philby when the Russian masterspy disappeared in January 1963. 'He got out one jump ahead of our eliminator,' one agent said. The news rocked Washington. Senator Frank Church, who headed one of the investigations, commented: 'Ours is not a wicked country and we cannot abide a wicked government.' More than 200 legislative bills were tabled to try to put the CIA under greater control. And the revelations caused a re-appraisal of a mystery death seven years earlier when NATO's top echelons were hit by a spy scandal.

It began on 27 September 1968, in a photographic shop in Bonn, the West German capital. At first the film being developed for a customer seemed routine – snaps of a family relaxing. Then the technician spotted saucy pictures of a naked blonde. But what really alarmed him were nine negatives of papers stamped: 'NATO – cosmic top secret'. It was the alliance's highest security classification. The darkroom assistant telephoned the police, who were instantly interested. For the roll of film had been left at the shop by Rear Admiral Hermann Luedke, the second most powerful man at Supreme Headquarters Allied Powers Europe (SHAPE), responsible for the logistics of NATO war supplies in Western Europe and the Middle East. He knew exactly where missiles, fuel, arms and rations were stored, and how they would be used in the event of fighting. He knew the locations of secret pipelines and minefields designed to thwart a Soviet invasion. And now the photographs had put his loyalty in question.

Counter-espionage officials, called in immediately, soon tracked down Luedke. As the film was being developed, he was sitting at a banquet where NATO generals were singing his praises to mark his retirement, at 57, through ill health. The spycatchers waited until the farewell ceremonies were over, then led the Rear Admiral to a side room and confronted him with the photographs. He readily identified the snaps of his family, blushed as he perused the pin-ups, then looked startled by the pictures of secret papers, which were accompanied by three close-ups of his car registration number. The incriminating pictures, the first 12 on the reel, were the only ones Luedke denied taking. At long interrogations that night and next day, his only explanation was that someone must be trying to frame him. He agreed to a search of his home outside Bonn, which unearthed nothing suspicious. Then, with official permission, he drove to SHAPE's offices at Mons, Belgium, to clear his desk. He told colleagues there he was going on a hunting holiday. They were almost the last people to see him alive.

At 16.30 on 8 October 1968, a farmer found the body of a man in olive-green hunting clothes slumped beside a car in the Immerath area of the Eifel Hills. It was Luedke. A soft-nosed bullet from his own Mauser rifle had killed him. And though the wound was at the base of his spine, a post-mortem examination ruled that nobody else was involved in the death. It was either suicide or an accident caused when the gun was carelessly thrown into the back seat of the car without its safety catch secured. That verdict stunned the local doctor who first examined the body. And author David Lewis, who tested the possibility while researching his book *Sexpionage*, claimed such a death was an impossibility. But if Luedke had been murdered, who had done it? And why?

The Rear Admiral's death was one of 13 which stunned NATO in the next fortnight. Five hours before his body was found, Major General Horst Wendland, deputy chief of West Germany's BND counter-espionage service, put a bullet through his brain in his Pullach office. Ten days later, Lieutenant Colonel Johannes Grimm followed his example at his desk in the German Defence Ministry, where he was responsible for war mobilization plans. Federal filing clerk Edeltraud Grapentin took an overdose of sleeping pills on 14 October. On the same day, senior Economics Ministry official Hans Heinrich Schenk hanged himself at his Cologne apartment. A week later the body of Defence Ministry worker Gerhard Boehm was pulled from the Rhine near Bonn. Police statements attributed all the suicides to personal problems,

---

Cuban leader Fidel Castro claims the American CIA have tried to kill him 60 times since he imposed Communism in Havana. Plots are said to include a box of poisoned cigars and a chocolate milkshake containing a delayed action poison. The latter failed only because the drink froze in the refrigerator.

health worries, despair at being passed over for promotion. But counter-intelligence forces of the NATO countries knew better. They linked the deaths to the disappearance of six known East German agents who fled behind the Iron Curtain after the arrival in the West of a Czech defector.

General Jan Sejna took advantage of the confusion in Prague caused by the Soviet invasion of August 1968 to escape. In return for asylum, he revealed the extent of KGB penetration of NATO's defences. The Russians, realizing their networks were in peril, decided to turn their loss into a propaganda victory. By showing that NATO was 'riddled by traitors', they could undermine public confidence and cause friction between the 14 member countries. Driving a wedge between America and Germany might weaken cooperation and efficiency in defence of the West. And Luedke was the perfect wedge.

The enthusiastic amateur photographer had suspected nothing when a beautiful young French girl invited him back to her apartment in the Rue St Honoré a few hours after meeting him in a Paris nightclub. She posed willingly for pictures before they made love, and they enjoyed several more evenings of passion in the spring of 1966. Then KGB agents confronted Luedke with snaps he had not taken. He was warned that the glossy record of his infidelity would be shown to his wife and five children unless he cooperated. Reluctantly he agreed to the initial request, for information of no great value. He was handed the incriminating sex negatives. But more photographs were taken of the transaction. Now the threat was that his NATO career would explode in his face unless he provided more secrets. For a year, the Russians made few demands. Then President De Gaulle ordered SHAPE out of France. Planners of NATO had to carry out a crash programme, transferring the offices, files and communications network of the alliance from Rocquencourt, near Paris, to new centres in Brussels and Mons. The USSR, alarmed at the disruption of its own lines of clandestine communication ordered Luedke to keep them in touch with every development and recruit new moles in Belgium.

By April 1967, the NATO top brass were installed in their new bases, but there was no let-up in the pressure on Luedke. Weapons research had now been added to his department, and the Kremlin wanted to know all about it. He was even instructed to show Soviet agents the homing device from the new Hawk guided missile. Under protest he took great risks to steal the machinery and display it at a hush-hush rendezvous. After an electronics expert examined it, Luedke was told to return the device. He refused, saying such action would be too dangerous. So the Russians dumped it on a village rubbish tip.

The strain of espionage affected Luedke's health, and he grasped doctors' advice of early retirement as a welcome escape from his trap. But the Soviets had not finished with him. An agent borrowed his Minox camera, replaced the half-used film and took incriminating pictures of year-old secret documents and Luedke's car number. There was no reason for the Rear Admiral to suspect subterfuge. When he again used the camera, the shot meter still stood at 12 frames exposed. He finished the reel by snapping his latest mistress and the family before dropping the film off to be developed, unwittingly sparking off the scandal that cost him his life.

At first the KGB were suspected of his murder. But that made no sense. Having taken the trouble to implicate Luedke as a spy, why would they shoot him before a trial which would generate embarrassing publicity for the West? Only the counter-espionage services of West Germany and America would gain from the assassination of the highest-ranked NATO traitor ever unmasked. And after the revelations of the Washington hearings in 1975, speculation grew that the BND or CIA had indeed taken the easiest way out of a political crisis to spare their own blushes.

Buster Crabb: the Disappearing Diver

Assassinations by British agents were banned in 1956 when Sir Dick White switched from MI5 to become MI6 spymaster. Ironically, the move was caused by an over-ambitious adventure to gain intelligence which went wrong – and resulted in the death of a British frogman.

Prime Minister Sir Anthony Eden had high hopes of thawing the cold war when Soviet leaders Nikolai Bulganin and Nikita Khruschev agreed to visit London in April 1956. He issued orders that no attempt should be made to spy on the cruiser *Ordzonikidze*, which was bringing the two Russians to Portsmouth. But Naval Intelligence and MI6 could not resist the opportunity. The military men installed radar in a cave in the cliffs at Dover and stationed a submarine on the sea bed to snoop on the sophisticated warship as it neared the coast. And MI6 accepted an offer from the war hero Lionel 'Buster' Crabb to dive under the cruiser to scrutinize its hull.

Crabb was an experienced and daring frogman. During World War 2 he had won the George Medal and OBE for removing limpet mines from British warships off Gibraltar. And though, at 46, he was out of condition, he was still full of courage and ready to face new challenges. On Tuesday 17 April, he booked into the Sallyport Hotel in the heart of Portsmouth's dockland with a mystery man who registered as Bernard Smith. He spent the next day making test dives in the harbour, and when the *Ordzonikidze* arrived on 19 April, he again slid into the water shortly after daybreak. He returned within minutes, complaining of difficulties with his breathing device. But after making adjustments, he swam away towards the cruiser. He was never seen alive again.

The *Ordzonikidze* and her two sister ships had sailed for home before the first offical news of Crabb's disappearance was released, a week after the event. A statement said he 'was presumed dead as a result of trials with certain underwater equipment'. When pressed to give more details in the House of Commons, an embarrassed Sir Anthony Eden declared: 'It would not be in the public interest to disclose the circumstances.' Such secretiveness gave rise to a mystery which deepened when police visited the Sallyport Hotel and tore from the register the page listing the arrival of Crabb and Smith.

On 9 June 1957, a headless corpse was washed up on the shore 11 km (7 miles) east of Portsmouth. It was wearing a frogman's suit similar to the one Crabb wore, and had scars and small peculiarities identified by Crabb's ex-wife as those of her former husband. The local coroner was satisfied the body was Crabb's, but the cause of death remained a problem. Then a German newspaper reported the alleged confession of a Russian sailor, that Crabb was held in a Moscow jail. Other reports said the frogman had defected to Russia – and when a picture of some Soviet seamen was published in a Moscow magazine, Crabb's ex-wife and a war-time colleague identified one of the men as Crabb.

But it was clear from the start that Soviet indignation at the foolhardy espionage attempt was not all it seemed. The Russian party mentioned seeing a frogman near their ships when they dined at the Admiralty on the evening of 19 April. And Radio Moscow broadcast that the diver was dead before the British government announced the probability. Then, in 1963, defector Anatoli Golitsin told the CIA that Soviet intelligence had known in advance of the Crabb swim, and that Russian frogmen were waiting for him in a special compartment in the side of the ship below the waterline.

As long as there was doubt about Crabb's fate in the public mind, Moscow could manipulate British embarrassment for propaganda purposes. And Whitehall's reluctance to clear the air about a clandestine operation carried out without official blessing only helped to blacken the diver's name with hints of treachery. In fact, it is almost certain Buster Crabb died as he had lived – a hero. Just over 20 years later, another British hero was killed on active secret service. But this time, the authorities eventually officially recognized his courage ...

Robert Nairac: the Lonely Hero

The Special Air Service regiment is Britain's foremost fighting force. Triumphs in seemingly impossible missions such as the ending of the Iranian embassy siege in London in May 1980 have helped create an aura of invincibility about the superbly-trained men with the motto: Who Dares Wins. David Stirling founded the regiment during the North Africa campaigns of World War 2 to carry out clandestine behind-the-lines raids. And it was a short step from sabotage to the espionage world of surveillance and subversion when post-war peace was interrupted by colonial insurrections. In the jungles of Malaysia and Borneo, and later in Aden, the SAS learned all the tricks of the spying trade. And when Ulster was plunged into sectarian violence after 1969, the ultra-secret servicemen were drafted in to help the more established intelligence agencies improve the flow of information and stem the bloodshed. They became the foe the Provisional IRA feared most, particularly in the notorious 'bandit country' of South Armagh. Keeping lonely vigils on windswept hillsides, making plain-clothes patrols to collect gossip from locals, and waging a constant psychological war on the terrorists, they played a big part in cutting the death rate dramatically. Then, in 1977, the IRA exacted terrible revenge.

Captain Robert Nairac was 29, officially an officer in the Grenadier Guards, and according to his family a 'volunteer for peace in Ireland'. Unofficially the bachelor from Stonehouse, Gloucestershire, son of a wealthy eye surgeon, was an undercover SAS man. He opted for intelligence work in 1974, five years after joining the Army, and was trained as an espionage agent by both the SAS and MI6. For months he worked on London building sites and drank in seedy pubs in Kilburn and Camden Town, watching his Irish-born fellow labourers, copying their speech to disguise the plummy accent developed by his education at Ampleforth College, Yorkshire, Oxford University, and Sandhurst Military College.

As a Guardsman, he could have settled for the quiet ceremonial life of sentry duty at Buckingham Palace and parades such as Trooping the Colour. But Nairac had a taste for more dangerous service. At first he was stationed with the Grenadiers' 2nd Battalion in Belfast, patrolling the Protestant Shankhill and Catholic Ardoyne areas. A colleague later recalled:

'He became something of an expert with the Fianna, the young

> **Russian leaders are said to be terrified of the products of their top poison-making laboratory, nicknamed the Kamera (Chamber). One KGB chief said: 'You just touch something by chance and there's your funeral.' For years Politburo members refused to shake hands with strangers because they learned of a lethal needle which could be concealed in diamond signet rings, injecting toxins which killed hours later.**

Catholics who are the natural breeding ground for the IRA, and the Tartan gangs who supply the various Protestant para-military organizations. He was known and respected throughout the Ardoyne. He could disperse a hostile crowd of several hundred with a few words to the ringleaders. He won over the support of most of the local inhabitants by finding out their problems and then getting the local authorities to take action.'

It was a classic espionage 'hearts and minds' ploy to isolate terrorists.

Later Nairac was posted to the IRA-dominated border country, the most dangerous part of Northern Ireland for the security forces. And he astonished locals by ingratiating himself not in the usual furtive manner of spies, but with a bold mixture of blarney and charm. In uniform and out of it, he called at local public houses and joined in rousing sing-songs of Republican anthems. He told those who deigned to talk to him that he was from the Ardoyne, and had joined the Army after a Protestant mob burned his mother's house. Hints of Catholic sympathies and an open good nature won him trust and respect from many who dare not openly express their weariness at the never-ending killings, and he built up a network of contacts who were prepared to tip-off the authorities about the routes by which arms and explosives were smuggled into Ulster from the Irish Republic.

Then, on the night of 14 May 1977, he left his headquarters at Bessbrook, a converted linen mill, and drove his red Triumph Toledo to The Three Steps, an inn at Drumintree, near Forkhill, South Armagh. He had called there the previous night, but left after a few beers. Now he walked into the bar again making a routine coded check call to base at 21.50 on his car radio. The calls, a standard safety precaution for intelligence agents, should have been made every 90 minutes. Nairac never made another.

It was a Saturday night and the bar was packed. A country and western band were the big attraction for most, but Nairac was keeping a rendezvous with two men. He was seen chatting to them at a table. He may have been trying to trace those responsible for the bomb assassination of the British ambassador, Christopher Ewart-Biggs, in Dublin some months earlier. Shortly before closing time, he left with the two men. Others followed. Nairac was never seen again.

At first light his abandoned car was found in the pub yard. Windows were smashed, radio aerials had been torn off, and a wing mirror was broken. Keys, cigarettes and other personal effects were scattered about. And there were other more significant clues to a violent struggle – blood stains which trailed 18 m (20 yd) down the road towards the Eire border 4.8 km (3 miles) to the south. Tip-offs from two motorists led detectives to a field near woods at Ravensdale, Co. Louth, in the Republic, where more blood stains were found along with strands of human hair. Tests proved that they were Nairac's – he had a rare blood type shared by only one person in 500 in Ulster. Then the IRA announced they had interrogated and executed the SAS man.

Secrecy has always shrouded SAS soldiers and their activities. Even medals for courage are awarded without naming their real regiment. At first the authorities strenuously denied that Nairac was an SAS agent. But as police in both Ulster and Eire rounded up his killers, the true story of the Grenadier Guardsman's heroism emerged. Liam Townson, 34 and unemployed, was jailed for life in Dublin after admitting that he had been summoned from a pub in Dundalk and told, 'There's a job to be done and you'll need some hardware.' He had been driven to the Ravensdale forest, picking up a gun from a hiding place in a wall near the border on the way. He found Nairac in the hands of at least seven men who had tortured him in an attempt to extract information. Once Nairac had fought his way free, only to be clubbed down with a wooden stave. 'He was a brave soldier,' Townson said. 'He told us nothing.'

Five other men, one of them only 17 years old, were jailed in Belfast for their part in the kidnap and killing of the courageous captain. Three others –

CIA boffins are said to have developed a shellfish toxin so deadly that one drop on the skin causes heart failure almost instantly. The poison later evaporates, leaving no trace. Other lethal CIA gadgets include an ash try which explodes when a cigarette is stubbed out, killing everyone within 3 m (10 ft), a cigar which contains a nerve gas gun triggered by touching the band, and a poison dart pistol concealed in a rolled newspaper carried under the arm and fired by pressure from the elbow.

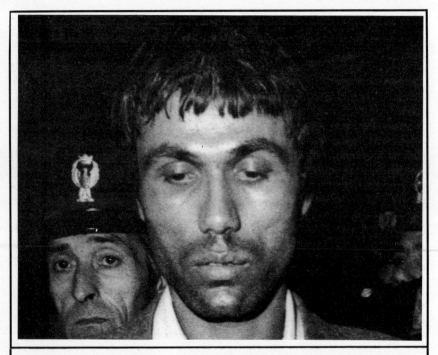

Turkish gunman Mehmet Ali Agca horrified the world on 13 May 1981, when he shot Pope John Paul II in Rome's St Peter's Square. The popular pontiff recovered after surgery, but then Agca, at first sullen and silent, provided new shocks. He claimed Bulgarian secret servicemen helped him in the assassination attempt – and said they were working on instructions from the KGB, who wanted the Pope dead because he was a figurehead to dissidents in his native Poland. Spokesmen in both Moscow and Sofia poured scorn on the allegations, saying Agca was diverting attention from his real backers. But police arrested Sergei Antonov, said to be at Agca's side during the shooting, after the Bulgarian's unlisted telephone number and a detailed description of his Rome apartment were provided by the gunman. Two other Bulgarians, both in Rome under diplomatic cover at the time of the attack, had left the city when Agca named them as fellow conspirators.

including the only man believed to know where Nairac's body was hidden – had fled abroad before police could interview them. Human remains believed to be Nairac's were unearthed in 1984.

On 1 May 1979, Nairac's parents and his sister went to Buckingham Palace to receive from the Queen the nation's highest decoration for gallantry in peacetime, the George Medal. The citation with it, the first formal admission that the captain was involved in surveillance work with the SAS, praised the outstanding contribution he had made during four tours of duty in Ulster, totalling 28 months.

Then came confirmation that at least seven men abducted him at Drumintree, 'despite fierce resistance', and took him across the border, where he was:

> 'subjected to a succession of exceptionally savage assaults in an attempt to extract information which would have put other lives and future operations at risk. These efforts to break Captain Nairac's will failed completely. Weakened as he was in strength, though not in spirit, by the brutality, he yet made repeated and spirited attempts to escape, but on each occasion was eventually overpowered by the weight of numbers against him.
>
> After several hours in the hands of his captors, Captain Nairac was callously murdered by a gunman of the Provisional IRA who had been summoned to the scene. Captain Nairac's exceptional courage and acts of the greatest heroism in circumstances of extreme peril showed devotion to duty and personal courage second to none.'

If the IRA hoped their execution would deter further spies, they were sadly mistaken. In September 1980, it was revealed that a mole within the terrorist ranks in South Armagh had tipped off the Eire police about a string of arms caches. A Royal Ulster Constabulary spokesman said: 'Southern security forces have seized more explosives along the border in the past week than in the last ten years.' The bomb material would have lasted Ulster Provisionals a year. In 1983 Northern Ireland security forces acquired a series of terrorist super-grasses whose information led to mass arrests. One refused to withdraw his evidence even after his father, young sister and wife were seized as hostages. Surprisingly, all three were later released unharmed. It was proof that Nairac's espionage successors were winning the psychological war. The spy so savagely slaughtered had not died in vain.

Chapter Eight

Middle East Spies

The Middle East has always been a vital battleground in the worldwide Soviet-NATO cold war. Russian superspies Kim Philby and George Blake both served in Beirut and Donald Maclean passed secrets from Cairo. But Israel's struggle for existence at the heart of the Arab states has produced equally astonishing espionage exploits...

The Daring Courage of Elie Cohen

The Jews learned the art of spying the hard way. Centuries of persecution, purges and pogroms developed in them a natural talent for survival in a hostile environment and the cunning ability to keep their real thoughts, feelings and intentions secret while finding out about those of their oppressors. Since Biblical times, Jews have been invaluable agents for every nation with espionage aspirations. Forty years ago, it was the underground activities of the Irgun and Haganah organizations which finally brought to reality the long-held dream of the Jewish homeland in Palestine. And since 1948, the secret services of tiny Israel have become the envy of the world.

Their efficiency has been honed out of necessity – no new state has ever had to fight so many wars against neighbours committed to crushing it – and a passionate patriotism unique among intelligence organizations. The exploits of Israeli agents have won admiration even from their enemies. And no one earned it more than the amazing Elie Cohen.

Cohen was the Egyptian-born son of Syrian parents. He worked as a book-keeper in Alexandria until 1956, when fear of an anti-Jewish backlash from President Nasser after the disastrous Anglo-French Suez invasion, and fighting between Israel and Egypt, made him decide to move to Tel Aviv. His quick brain and superb memory quickly brought him to the attention of Mossad, the overseas arm of the Israeli secret services.

His training was thorough and ruthlessly professional. Israeli agents are pushed to the limits of physical endurance to test their ability to withstand torture. And Cohen's cover also had to be perfect. For he was to be installed in Damascus, capital of Israel's most consistently hostile neighbour, Syria. He was given a new identity, Kamel Amine Tabet, a Syrian Moslem. And to make his new character convincing, he had to learn a new life story involving birth in the Lebanese capital, Beirut, and emigration to Argentina. Cohen perfected his Syrian accent talking to businessmen in Jerusalem, then flew to Buenos Aires via Zurich.

With discreet Mossad back-up, providing an apartment and ample funds, Cohen quickly established himself in the Syrian community as an ardent, Israeli-hating patriot. He made friends with influential people inside and outside the Syrian embassy in Buenos Aires, and impressed them with generous donations to Arab charities. By early 1962, Mossad felt he was ready for the next step, and ordered him to Damascus. He flew to Italy, took a boat to Beirut, and bribed his way through a Syrian border customs post – he did not want prying officials to find his miniature radio transmitter, codes and invisible inks.

Cohen had no time to follow the classic KGB ploy of lying low and not attracting attention. Tel Aviv wanted results fast, and that meant risking exposure by establishing contacts ostentatiously. Cohen moved into a luxurious villa and began trading as an import-export dealer. He told everyone he was a Ba'ath Party convert who had come home to help his country, and he backed his words with cash drawn on an American bank. He impressed local big-wigs by importing expensive French mink coats as gifts for their wives. At first, the only danger came from marriage brokers, intent on finding him a suitable bride. Cohen politely declined all offers. Not only did he already have a wife in Israel, but he needed his bachelor privacy in Syria to radio secrets to Tel Aviv.

And there was much to tell. His fierce patriotism earned him the chance to give talks on Radio Damascus, aimed at Syrians overseas in Spanish-speaking countries. He accepted at once. He could now learn from the inside about the Ministry of Information, which provided basic material for the broadcasts, and slip pre-arranged code words into the chats for Israeli ears only. These supplemented his clandestine radio transmissions and the secret messages he smuggled out in 'exports' to Mossad in Argentina.

> **An audacious plan by Israeli intelligence to try to change American Middle East policy in 1954 was foiled by a traitor. Israel was worried that the United States was becoming too friendly with Egypt, and a scheme was devised to frighten off the White House by planting bombs in strategic American and British buildings in Cairo and Alexandria. But counter-espionage forces were waiting, and captured the 11-strong Israeli team of agents. One of them, Hans Hoffman, who operated on a British passport under the name Paul Frank, had revealed the whole operation to Colonel Osman Nouri, the brilliant Cairo head of military intelligence. Two of the saboteurs were executed, one committed suicide rather than talk, and eight were jailed. It took years for Israel to build up an effective new spy ring in Egypt.**

Cohen made a point of urging stronger defences against Israel whenever he met important people from the ruling military junta. Anxious to prove that his fears were groundless, they gave him conducted tours of the defences on the Golan Heights, and revealed a network of underground tunnels along the Israeli border. Soon senior army officers made Cohen's villa a regular meeting place, particularly after he began to provide girls for them, and tongues wagged freely in the relaxed atmosphere.

Cohen ingratiated himself so well that he became an honorary major in the army, and was given a responsible position in the Ba'ath party. This enabled him to accompany the Prime Minister on visits to other Arab capitals, including Cairo, where he sat in on talks between leaders and their military experts. Soon the successful spy had so much material that he had to get back to Israel to unburden his memory. Using a business trip to Argentina as his cover, he flew to Buenos Aires, stayed a few days, then flew to Europe, and slipped unnoticed back to Tel Aviv. Israel now knew exactly the strength of the Syrian forces facing her, and the intentions of their leaders, as well as the plans and attitudes of Syria's allies.

A Ba'ath party coup soon after Cohen's return to Damascus early in 1963 put the informer in an even stronger position. Several of his closest friends were now ministers, and he was able to keep the Israelis in touch with all the latest government thinking, together with news of arms purchases and army dispositions.

But such staggering success in so short a time sowed the seeds of its own destruction. Perhaps over-confident, Cohen allowed himself to be photographed in the official group when he accompanied the United Arab Republic's commander-in-chief on an inspection of border military posts. Then the Voice of Israel radio station broadcast some secret facts Cohen had provided. It was a stupid mistake, alerting the Syrians to a spy in their midst. And when, months later, Egyptian secret police told their Syrian counterparts that an old schoolfriend had identified Kamel Amine Tabet as an Egyptian Jew from the photograph published in newspapers, the game was over.

Though aware of the spy hunt, Cohen courageously continued to file reports to Tel Aviv. One of his last transmissions told of sabotage teams being trained for infiltration. And he was using the radio on the morning counterespionage men burst into his villa and arrested him.

The repercussions of the arrest were enormous. Cohen was tried in secret, not so much for security reasons as to save embarrassment among Syria's rulers and their furious Arab allies. Two French advocates briefed by Israel were not allowed to defend him, or appeal against the inevitable death sentence. Their protests at this 'defiance of all moral rules' was ignored, as was Israel's unprecedented, top secret offer of army lorries, tractors, medical supplies, ten Syrian spies and more than a million dollars in exchange for one life. Elie Cohen was publicly hanged under floodlights in Damascus's Martyrs Square at Midnight on 18 May 1965. His body, mutilated by torture, was buried in the city, and all Israeli requests for its return were rejected.

The master spy's exploits led to the collapse of the government. Cabinet ministers who had befriended him were hounded out of office. Sixty army officers were arrested, and 17 executed for compromising the safety of the state. But the real damage to Syria only became apparent in 1967 during the Six Day War, when Israeli troops quickly routed the forces that had taunted them so long from the 'impregnable' Golan Heights.

Wolfgang Lotz: the Champagne Spy

While Elie Cohen was establishing himself in Damascus, an equally ingenious and extraordinary Israeli spy was winning acceptance in the upper echelons of Egyptian high society in Cairo. For four years Wolfgang Lotz, a German-born Jew, conned police, army and espionage chiefs in Gamal Nasser's republic by wining and dining them in a way which earned him the nickname 'The Champagne Spy'. And after sending back a stream of priceless information which helped Israel win the Six Day War, he survived to join the victory celebrations in Tel Aviv.

During the 1950s, Israel was increasingly concerned at the growing number of ex-Nazis hired by Egypt to work on fighter aircraft and rocket missiles. It was clear Nasser intended some devastating strike against his Jewish neighbours. Painstaking detective work by Israeli secret agents all over the world and sympathetic intelligence men in America, France and Germany helped pinpoint the 400 scientists, technicians and engineers involved, and how they were hired. But Israel needed somebody inside Egypt to find out how the work was progressing. It did not take Mossad chiefs long to locate the ideal candidate.

Wolfgang Lotz was the son of a Mannheim theatre impresario and an actress, so playing roles was in his blood. After his father died, his mother emigrated to Palestine in 1933. At 16, Lotz first tasted undercover work with the Haganah, fighting to protect Jewish villagers, and during World War 2 he served in the British Army as a Commando, seeing action in the desert battles against Rommel, and picking up Egyptian dialects while stationed in the Suez area. Then he joined the new Israeli army, winning promotion to major after distinguished campaigns in the 1948 war of independence and the 1956 Sinai battles. By 1960 he had proved himself ice-cool under pressure. He was fluent in English, Arabic and German. He was also blond and German-looking. He was just what the Israeli spy masters needed.

Lotz agreed to play the part of a pro-Nasser ex-Nazi who hated Jews. After intensive training in the tricks of the espionage trade – coded messages, invisible ink etc – he was sent back to Germany to perfect his cover. He travelled from city to city, familiarizing himself with the latest slang, and the names of sporting and TV stars, for use in small talk. Since he had been born in Germany, his life story was based on his real name and birth certificate. It was not too difficult to pretend he had fought with Rommel during the war – he had fought the battles, but on the other side – and to hide the fact that he had left Germany in 1933, an 11-year stay in Australia was invented.

Armed with letters of introduction from carefully cultivated new friends met on his return to Germany, Lotz sailed to Egypt as a tourist in January 1961. Posing as a breeder of top class horses, he asked staff at his Nile-side hotel where he could go riding. They directed him to the Cavalry Club, an exclusive haunt of police and army chiefs. On his first visit, he complimented police general Youssef Ghorab on his horsemanship. Ghorab, delighted with the flattery, invited him to dinner next night. There he was introduced to other influential guests as 'Germany's top horse breeder'. Everyone was enthusiastic when Lotz said he was considering opening a stud farm in Egypt. And within weeks he was on close terms not only with Ghorab, but with Colonel Abdul Rahman, deputy head of Egyptian military intelligence, General Fouad Osman, chief of security for Egypt's rocket sites, and many of the Germans working on Nasser's secret projects. He returned to Europe to report to his Mossad masters.

By late 1961, Lotz was back in Egypt, with 17 trunks of luggage and a Volkswagen car. A police colonel escorted him down the gangway from his ship at Alexandria to a typical Arab embrace from General Ghorab. His trunks were waved through customs, and a police escort gave him VIP passage off the crowded quayside. The new German immigrant brought expensive presents for his new friends – stereo record players, tape recorders, coffee makers, food mixers. He also imported something he told no one about – a secret radio transmitter hidden in the heel of one of his riding boots. And, to the delight of the Egyptians, he had acquired a wife.

Marrying Waltraudt Neumann, a busty, blonde who looked typically

Counter-espionage forces in Israel have special problems
because of the large number of Arab citizens legally living
there, and the ever-open door to immigrants from
oppression elsewhere. The Soviet Union has used 'refugees'
as spies. Perhaps the most effective was Israel Beer, an
Austrian who fled to Palestine from the Nazis in 1938, and
earned a high reputation as an Israeli freedom fighter and a
soldier for the new state. He became the nation's official
military historian, with access to all the archives, and was
principal aide to the Army Chief of Staff, and later Defence
Minister David Ben Gurion. Such posts involved liaison with
NATO countries, and enabled Beer to provide Moscow with
top secrets about Israel and Europe. He was arrested in 1962
after the Israelis were given information from the British
debriefing of spy George Blake, and the CIA's questioning of
Polish defector Michal Goleniewski. A Tel Aviv court jailed
Beer for ten years, but he died in prison four years later.

German, was something of a feat for Lotz because he was already married, to
an Israeli girl, the mother of his two children. It took delicate persuasion from
Mossad to convince her that Lotz's 'wedding ceremony' in Munich was
purely a marriage of convenience, necessary to perfect his cover in Egypt.
And Waltraudt proved an invaluable ally for Lotz, helping him host the
lavish parties at which champagne loosened tongues, and asking questions
which, from Lotz, would have been highly impertinent and suspicious. The
Egyptians treated her like a queen, and many would do almost anything for
her.

The Lotzes established their stud farm in the fashionable Cairo suburb of
Zamalek, on an island in the Nile, and lived first in a nearby apartment, then
in a luxurious eight-bedroom villa in Gizeh. They slipped easily into the
upper class social round, riding in the morning, lazing by the Cavalry Club
swimming pool, sipping cocktails at sunset, partying almost every evening.
Lotz stabled some horses at a riding school in Abbasia, and established the
habit of climbing a tower by the school's race track to watch them being
exercised. From the tower, he also had a perfect view of the Egyptian army's
biggest tank depot next door, and could see when tanks were mobilized for
action, and which direction they were sent. Livestock deals were also a good
excuse for Lotz's periodic trips back to Germany, to pass on what he learned
to his spymasters. And his high-up contacts helped him learn a lot.

General Ghorab introduced him to the governor of the Suez Canal zone, and all three toured military installations there in the governor's car. General Osman invited him to inspect rocket bases in the Sinai and Negev deserts, and even posed for a portrait in front of one of the rockets on its launching pad. He believed Lotz was just a keen amateur photographer. Once, when Lotz and Waltraudt took a chance and drove their car down a prohibited road in the desert between Cairo and Ismailia to check out reports of a secret base there, guards who arrested them were so impressed with the names Lotz gave as people who would vouch for him that the couple were entertained to lunch at the base by the commanding officer.

Top Egyptian army men felt free to share ultra-secret plans at Lotz's parties. Colonel Anwar Sadat, later to succeed Nasser as president, was among the guests coaxed by Lotz to chat about Cairo's intentions against Israel, and the prospects of concerted military action by Middle East nations. Germans working on the feared rocket projects were equally forthcoming. Lulled into a false sense of security by Lotz's pretended nostalgia for the Third Reich, they moaned about technical hitches and the problems of working with Arabs. Lotz was able to monitor progress on the weapons, and pinpoint key workers who were targets later of an Israeli terror campaign involving letter bombs, anonymous phone threats and gun-point warnings. Lotz was so close to the German workers, and so trusted by the Egyptians, that he was asked by General Osman to report on some of the immigrants. When Lotz alleged that one brilliant scientist had no sympathy for Nasser and was working only for the money, the German's six-year contract was cancelled and he was expelled.

Then, quite suddenly, the bubbly life of Israel's champagne superspy went flat. He shrugged off a dinner party conversation in which a West German embassy attaché said he could not remember Lotz being a member of Rommel's Afrika Korps. But on 22 February 1965, counter-espionage agents were waiting for him and Waltraudt when they returned to their villa after spending the weekend with General Ghorab. The Egyptians had discovered the couple's new radio transmitter, a larger and more powerful model concealed in a pair of bathroom scales. And they had a complete dossier of their messages to Tel Aviv over three years. Their praise – 'You were the best spy ever to work in Egypt' – was small consolation to Lotz for being caught.

The Egyptians later claimed that Lotz gave himself away through carelessness. They said security men checking every house along the route to be used for an official visit by East German leader Walter Ulbricht had been let into Lotz's villa by a servant, and found the radio and codes lying about. A more likely explanation for the spy's demise is that Lotz was 'blown' by one of the Russian agents who infiltrated West German intelligence in the 1960s. The Israelis needed German help to establish Lotz's bona fides in Egypt, and later cooperated closely with Bonn in the hope that the government there would persuade Germans not to work for Nasser. And by 1965, Russia was anxious to impress the Egyptian leader.

Once he realized that the game was up, Lotz concentrated on saving his own life and protecting Waltraudt. He knew that if the Egyptians discovered he was an Israeli, he would be executed, just as Elie Cohen was a few months later in Syria. In his favour was the fact that, unusually for a Jew, he was uncircumcised. Both he and Waltraudt were tortured, but both maintained they were West Germans, and Lotz convinced his captors that his 'wife' had little to do with the espionage. Shortly before the trial, he grabbed the chance of a propaganda TV appearance to declare: 'If the Israelis want to spy in Egypt, they should send their own people there.' It confirmed his non-Jewishness in Arab eyes, while telling Tel Aviv that his cover had not been broken.

Though playing the role of the remorseful agent saved him from death, Lotz was still sentenced to 25 years hard labour in the notoriously tough Tura penitentiary near Cairo. Waltraudt was jailed for three years as an accomplice. West German consul officials visited both, helping to maintain the fiction of their nationality. And Bonn was also involved in the delicate negotiations which resulted in Lotz being freed on 3 February 1968. He and nine Israeli servicemen were exchanged for 500 of the 4,400 Egyptian prisoners-of-war held by Israel.

The Cairo authorities insisted as part of the deal that Lotz be returned to West Germany as a German citizen. And he was duly handed his airline tickets to exile by the West German consul. But when the Lufthansa flight to Frankfurt stopped over in Athens, Lotz and Waltraudt left the plane and secretly returned to Tel Aviv, unsung heroes whose information had played a crucial part in Israel's stunning Six Day War victory eight months earlier.

A German SS officer became an Egyptian spy in the Israeli army after a despicable trick. Lieutenant Ulrich Schonhaft escaped retribution for Nazi atrocities at the end of World War 2 by buying the identity papers of Gabriel Sussmann, a Jewish concentration camp victim. Taken to Palestine with other refugees, he joined the Israeli army and impressed officers with his enthusiasm and discipline. But Schonhaft was detected sending secret information to Cairo, and his second anti-Jewish campaign ended with a seven-year jail sentence before expulsion back to Germany.

How a Bunch of Flowers Trapped Eichmann

One of the most callous war criminals of all time was trapped by an alert spy – because of a bouquet of flowers. Ricardo Klement bought the blooms in the Suarez suburb of Buenos Aires, Argentina, on 21 March 1960. Just over two years later, he died on the gallows in Tel Aviv, Israel. For the bouquet was final proof that Klement was Adolf Eichmann, the Nazi most hated by Jews all over the world. And it ended an astonishing 15-year hunt involving the espionage organisations of three nations.

Eichmann was the SS lieutenant-colonel with overall responsibility for Hitler's extermination of 6 million Jews. At the end of the war, he destroyed his records and personal file, burned all his photographs, and disguised himself as a Luftwaffe private. American forces who arrested him in May 1945 were not too interested in ordinary airmen, and in the confusion Eichmann managed to slip out of sight – but not out of Jewish minds.

The intelligence services of the new state of Israel were at first too busy with its baptism of fire – the 1948 war of independence against Arab neighbours – to settle old scores. But in 1950 a Mossad agent in the North African port of Tangier reported that 30 high-ranking Nazi fugitives had fled Europe via Spain and Italy – and one, Ricardo Clementi, had headed for Latin America on refugee papers issued by Vatican City authorities.

Then, in 1957, a German half-Jew who settled in Argentina after going blind in Dachau concentration camp told German secret service men investigating Nazi escapes that a schoolmate of his daughter had made anti-semitic statements praising Hitler for murdering Jews. The boy's name was Nikolaus Klement. And when the girl described his father, the ex-prisoner was convinced he was Eichmann. His hunch was reported to Dr Fritz Bauer, chief prosecutor in the German state of Hesse. Dr Bauer, himself a Jew, passed the news secretly to Tel Aviv, giving the Israelis Klement's address: 4261 Chacabuco Street, Olivos, Buenos Aires.

It was confirmation of a lead Mossad had established for itself. Espionage chiefs knew Eichmann's wife Veronika, who disappeared from her home in Linz, Austria, with her two children, at Easter 1952, would have to return to Vienna to renew her passport. When she eventually turned up, Mossad men were waiting, and shadowed her day and night before losing her trail in Argentina.

Adolf Eichmann

Israel's supreme spymaster, Isser Harel, now took charge of the Eichmann operation. His team had two priorities: to establish beyond all doubt that Klement was Eichmann – seizing the wrong man would make Israel an international laughing stock – and to do it without alerting their target, or Nazi sympathisers who might help him to escape. Delicate negotiations with the Argentinian secret service revealed that Buenos Aires knew Klement's real identity, but the authorities were prepared to let Israel deal with him quietly to avoid the embarrassment of extradition proceedings, which would disclose to the world that Argentina was knowingly harbouring war criminals.

Revenge was not the only Israeli motive. Anti-communist hysteria in America had led to a neo-Fascist backlash, and some people were already re-appraising Hitler's regime, and claiming his oppression of the Jews had been exaggerated. The world was beginning to forget. For the same reason, simple assassination of Eichmann would not do. Simon Wiesenthal, the concentration-camp survivor who had later dedicated his life to tracking down war criminals, said: 'If you kill him, the world will never learn what he did. There must be an accounting, a record for history.'

Mossad watchers in Argentina began a discreet round-the-clock surveillance of Klement and his family. Long-range photographs were sent back to Tel Aviv to be shown to death camp survivors. None could positively identify Eichmann. It had been so long ago, they had seen him only fleetingly.

The longer the watch continued, the greater became the chances of discovery by ex-Nazis or Argentinians not in the know. Then came the breakthrough. Klement was photographed buying flowers on 21 March as he left his work at the Mercedes Benz factory in Suarez. He was still carrying them when he arrived home in Olivos. One of the watchers made the vital connection between the date and the action. 21 March was Eichmann's wedding anniversary. If Klement was Mrs Eichmann's second husband, he would hardly celebrate his predecessor's special day.

Harel now had the go-ahead to put into operation what was later described as the best-organized kidnapping ever made by a secret service. With the Argentinians agreeing to a neutral role, neither overtly helping nor hindering the operation, he hand-picked an 11-strong team, including a doctor. Some of them made their own way to Buenos Aires by different routes, and established two safe houses, one for holding Eichmann, the other in case the first was discovered.

The rest of the team arrived in Argentina disguised as air crew on an El Al plane which flew in on 12 May 1960, carrying top Israeli diplomats to help celebrate the 150th anniversary of Argentina's independence. By that time, Eichmann was already in Israeli hands. Three agents bundled him into a car seconds after he stepped off the bus from work on the evening of 11 May. He was rushed to the safe house, stripped, and examined carefully for distinguishing marks. The appendicitis scar, the scar above the left eyebrow, and the SS giveaway, the blood group tattoo under the left armpit, were all there. The spies had their man. A pre-arranged code alerted Tel Aviv to the good news.

When the El Al plane was ready to leave, Eichmann was drugged, and his guards, posing as nurses and relatives, drove him to Buenos Aires airport with forged papers showing him to be a car crash victim with head injuries who was just fit enough to travel, but could not be disturbed. The cover worked perfectly. Within 24 hours, the man the Jews hated most was in Tel Aviv.

Israel was scrupulous in ensuring that the full procedure of the law was carried through, but the result of the trial, which began on 12 December 1961, was never in doubt. Eichmann was convicted of 15 charges of deporting and causing the death of millions of Jews, and being a party to the murder of thousands of gipsies and 91 children. He was hanged on 31 May 1962.

Chapter Nine

Space Age Spies

In the second half of the 20th century, machines and computers began taking over jobs previously done by men. Silicon-chip technology was said to be more reliable, more cost efficient, capable of more. The espionage industry was no exception. But occasionally, human spies find ways of hitting back ...

Secret Watchers of Land, Sea and Sky

Les Brown could hardly believe his bleary eyes. There on his doorstep stood a policeman and an RAF helicopter pilot in full flying gear. Their frowns were a surprise at 06.00, but the reason they had dragged Les from his bed was even more astonishing. Helicopters and ships had spent the night trying to track down the source of a mysterious SOS signal. Radar operators at Toulouse, France, pinpointed the bleep to the Firth of Clyde region of Scotland, and staff at Pitreavie search and rescue station, Fife, and the Faslane nuclear submarine base had now narrowed the target down – to Les's humble home at Erskine, near Glasgow. The culprit was a faulty radio distress beacon stored on top of the wardrobe in Les's spare bedroom. The £10 device, destined for a fishing boat Les was working on, had sparked a hunt costing nearly £20,000, and wife Marilyn told journalists: 'The only way to describe how we feel is totally embarrassed.'

Newspapers had fun with the story on 16 July 1983. But it had a significance far beyond mere amusement. For first news of the SOS came from a Russian space satellite. And its ability to pick out so tiny a target from miles up in orbit was devastating proof of the frightening effectiveness of spy-in-the-sky surveillance. Within six weeks, a far more serious event showed that the West, too, has electronic eyes and ears trained on every part of the globe. When Russian MiG fighters blasted Korean Airline's Flight 007 and its 269 innocent passengers out of the night skies over Sakhalin island, between the Soviet mainland and Japan, an American intelligence worker said: 'Almost certainly we knew before Moscow what the MiG pilots were doing and saying.' It was priceless ammunition in an international crisis that appalled the world. And it spelt out exactly why space age technology is now responsible for 85 per cent of modern espionage fact-gathering. The most valuable spies are no longer the human agents, of the CIA, KGB and MI6, but sophisticated satellites, snooping ships, ultra-sensitive land eavesdropping stations and complex banks of computers working round the clock.

The West's main security watchdogs are America's National Security Agency (NSA), based at Fort Meade, a 4.45 ha (11 acre) site in lush Maryland farmland 48 km (30 miles) north of Washington, and Britain's Government Communications Headquarters, at Cheltenham, Gloucestershire. They employ around 140,000 people and cost an estimated £15 billion a year to run. And according to a former NSA employee, they can 'maintain a moment-by-moment pattern of just about everything that is happening in the world that could be of military or political significance.' A man who worked at GCHQ said: 'They can track down anything that moves, from a tea cup to an atom bomb.' That ability comes from looking at the globe from every angle.

Spies have been in the skies since the 19th century, when wise generals sent manned hot-air ballons over enemy lines to assess strengths and tactics. During World War 2, cameras added a new dimension to the all-seeing eyes of aircraft pilots, culminating in the 1950s in high-altitude U2 jet flights over Russia by American airmen. But on 5 May 1960, U2 pilot Francis Gary Powers was shot down over Sverdlovsk in a blaze of embarrassing publicity. Months earlier another U2 plane had been forced down. Its crew of eight were never heard of again. President Eisenhower banned further flights, and in 1963, shortly after Powers was freed in exchange for Soviet masterspy Rudolf Abel, the first unmanned satellite went into orbit. Within two years the space snoops had proved their worth, detecting plutonium production at an Inner Mongolia factory no Western agent could reach, and alerting America to the first nuclear bomb test by China. Satellites have since been refined until their espionage potential is amazing, as the Erskine SOS and the storm over Flight 007 showed.

Cameras 321 km (200 miles) up can focus on objects no more than 30.4 cm (1 ft) long. Those aboard US Big Bird satellites can make out car registration numbers and newspaper headlines with their 243.8 cm (96 in) lenses. They can tell whether human targets are wearing spectacles. Infrared detectors pinpoint underground missile sites by measuring changes in earth temperature. Sound sensors intercept radio, telephone and microwave communications. American orbiters have picked up radio-telephone conversations between Politburo members heading for Kremlin meetings in separate limousines. Other satellites are programmed to locate rocket plumes, nuclear fall-out and submarines. Some can even feed false signals to Soviet technicians testing missiles.

Aerial espionage is supported by piracy of secrets on and under the high seas, Moscow masterminds the movements of hundreds of innocent-looking trawlers and merchant ships. They call at Western ports to collect information. They tour sensitive coastlines and trail NATO warships on exercises. In early 1982 some followed Britain's task force to the South Atlantic for the re-taking of the Falkland Islands. A year later a merchant ship moored a mile off Florida to watch US scientists test a Trident missile. An American observer said it had 'so many electronic masts and dishes it risked capsizing.'

America's fleet also includes spy ships which anchor off troublespots to

> According to NATO intelligence experts, up to 20,000
> Communist agents flooded into the West during the early
> 1980s with instructions to buy, beg, borrow or steal
> technology secrets. Russia was trying to catch up with
> Western advances in electronics without wasting time and
> resources. Posing as students and businessmen, the agents
> openly bought sophisticated children's computer games so
> Moscow could study how they were programmed. Bogus
> shops and businesses were started, ordering high-technology
> products which were later shipped behind the Iron Curtain.
> Targets which could not be bought were stolen from
> factories and exhibitions. And innocently-used space age
> gadgets were adapted for use in missile guidance and
> detection systems. A CIA spokesman said: 'We are being
> robbed of hundreds of millions of taxpayers' money spent to
> obtain our hard-earned technological lead over the Soviet
> bloc. They have developed sophisticated military systems
> that rival our own without the heavy expenditure in
> research and development that normally accompany such
> gains.'

eavesdrop on radio and telephone traffic. One was attacked by Israeli jets in the Mediterranean during the 1967 Six Day War. A year later came an even greater disaster. Four North Korean gunboats seized the USS *Pueblo* in international waters on 23 January 1968. The crew of 82, busy monitoring shipping and radar installations along the coast, were held hostage for 11 months in what a Czech defector later described as a carefully-planned Kremlin conspiracy to humiliate America, discourage US spying and show North Korean leaders that Russia could be a more powerful ally than China. The plot succeeded beyond Moscow's wildest dreams. Besides the propaganda coup, the Communists acquired details of America's Pacific operations and codes which enabled the KGB to read thousands of previously indecipherable messages stored on tape. A US inquiry recommended disciplinary action against Commander Lloyd Mark Bucher and his chief intelligence officer. But Navy Secretary John H. Chafee ruled: 'They have suffered enough.'

Sea snooping also goes on beneath the waves. Both Sweden and Norway dropped depth charges on suspected Soviet submarines prowling the depths along their shores during the early 1980s. And in June 1983 sophisticated acoustic monitoring equipment was discovered on the ocean bed off America's west coast. It was a Russian device to track the movements of US nuclear submarines – but no one knew how it had been installed, and how long it had been there.

On land, too, electronic surveillance has been refined to astounding levels. NSA and GCHQ run a network of 2,000 ultra-sensitive listening stations stretching round the globe, from Alaska to Australia, from Belize to Botswana, from Canada to Cyprus. There are even two in northern China, allowed to operate by the Communists in exchange for sharing information on Soviet troop movements. During the shooting down of Flight 007 in August 1983, those stations, plus others in Taiwan, Hong Kong Japan and South Korea were tuning in along with satellites to the terse comments of MiG pilots and their ground controllers.

Information from all these eyes and ears pour into the spy nerve centres of NSA and GCHQ at a rate of more than a million words a second. At Fort Meade and Cheltenham, computer banks decode, translate, collate and analyze intercepts instantly. Electronic brains capable of scanning four million characters a second, and reading and indexing any newspaper in the time it takes to pronounce its title, are programmed to spot key words and sound the alert whenever anything out of the ordinary happens. Fort Meade alone pours out 40 tons of documents a day with detailed breakdowns of worldwide diplomatic, political, military and economic data for the White House and Washington spymasters.

Up-to-date briefings on happenings anywhere in the world are on the desks of those who need to know in minutes.

Western watchers claim to know instantly whenever a Warsaw Pact missile is launched, when a plane takes off, when an army moves. They can recognize every Iron Curtain pilot from his call sign. NSA and GCHQ learned in advance, partly through increased radio traffic, of the 1962 Cuban missiles crisis and the 1968 Soviet invasion of Czechoslovakia. British listening outposts helped America monitor enemy intentions during the Vietnam war, and the US returned the compliment by passing on Argentinian messages during the Falklands confrontation. And when Britain negotiated Common Market entry, knowledge of the attitudes of other European governments was more than useful in the bargaining.

A GCHQ chief once wrote to his NSA counterpart: 'Between us we have ensured that the blankets and sheets are more tightly tucked around the bed in which our sets of people lie.'

But in 1982 that confidence was rudely shattered. The world learned that a red had sneaked into the bed, and all the latest space technology can be rendered irrelevant by one small human cog in the great intelligence machine . . .

Geoffrey Prime: the Most Dangerous Mole of All?

Geoffrey Arthur Prime, described by his own defence counsel as a desperately lonely, totally inadequate sexual and social misfit, was probably more valuable as a spy to the Kremlin than even Kim Philby. The priceless secrets he betrayed caused the greatest crisis of confidence in the Anglo-American intelligence alliance for 30 years. Jailing him for 38 years at the Old Bailey, Lord Chief Justice Lane said he had ruthlessly inflicted incalculable and irrevocable harm on Britain and its friends. And Attorney General Sir Michael Havers, asking for part of the hearing to be held in secret, said: 'To convey the extreme gravity of what Prime did and the information he passed would be prejudicial to the national safety.'

Yet, incredibly, the insignificant-looking loner who almost single-handedly put Western defences in peril for nearly 14 years was caught only because of his perverted interest in young girls. And for hoodwinking the White House and compromising the most complex and costly surveillance system ever devised, he received just £7,000 from his Moscow paymasters. One man who worked with him said : 'When I think of the information that went across his desk, I break out into a cold sweat.' For Prime, orderly and precise, was able to keep the Soviet Union one step ahead of its rivals in the deadliest arms race of all time. And ironically, it was the British government which started him on the espionage trail.

Prime, the son of a Staffordshire copper wire worker, was called up for national service in 1956. Life as an RAF storeman was dull, but at least it offered escape from an unhappy childhood scarred by a sexual assault from an adult relative. After his two compulsory years, Prime signed on for a voluntary ten-year stint as an airman. But his RAF career never got off the ground. His aptitude for languages made him ideal for intelligence work, and he was sent to a forces college in Scotland to study Russian and German.

This equipped him to join the eavesdropping teams which tune in to Soviet communications. At Cheadle, Cheshire, he helped plot Russian air movements by monitoring instructions to pilots. In Kenya he listened to radio transmissions to and from Moscow-backed guerrillas. And in 1964 he was drafted to the cold war front-line at RAF Gatow, West Berlin. Part of his duties was to check Radio Moscow broadcasts. Kenya's fading colonial system, with its seeming exploitation of natives, had disturbed him. Now Moscow's messages developed his left-wing sympathies. He later said they provided what he longed for, 'something to believe in'. In January 1968 he slipped a note to a Communist border guard at a Berlin Wall checkpoint. Weeks later he found a metal cylinder strapped to the door of his car. Inside were directions to Friedrichstrasse station, where KGB agents code-named Igor and Valya would contact him.

If the Russians had any doubts about Prime's sincerity, he soon set their minds at ease. He was more than eager to please. He told them all he knew about RAF Gatow's activities, providing photo-copies of the base's internal telephone directory. He also revealed the secrets of SWAMP, a device which converted Soviet radar transmissions into an electronic display to chart the movements of Warsaw Pact planes. Moscow had been confident that its jamming of NATO radar kept flights hidden. Now they foiled the plane-trackers by changing radar frequencies.

When Prime's RAF contract ended in September 1968, Igor and Valya encouraged him to apply for a Foreign Office job back home. He approached the Joint Technical Language Service, an innocuous-sounding organization which translates, collates and analyzes intercepted Eastern bloc messages. His outstanding linguistic skills made him a perfect candidate, and he had no trouble obtaining security clearance for secret work. Having recruited and installed their mole, the KGB set about training him.

Prime was taken to East Germany for lessons about invisible ink,

---

Soviet spymasters rarely miss a trick in their efforts to keep informed. In March 1982 it was revealed that KGB men and tank commanders were touring Western Europe posing as drivers of juggernauts. Austrian police arrested one who had his cab radio tuned into their army's High Command network, and was trying to crack the code used on a miniature computer. In Holland, lorry drivers were spotted testing the depths of rivers, searching for shallow crossing points for tanks and transport vehicles. Two months later a strange group of tourists booked into Antwerp for a package holiday. They spent four days admiring sophisticated lock gates along the river Scheldt, and taking pictures of the busy Belgian port. Only later was it learned that the 25 burly East Germans were members of a sabotage commando unit, spying out the land in case the port had to be crippled one day.

Geoffrey Prime

microdots, miniature cameras and coded 'squirt' radio transmissions – speeded-up messages broadcast in seconds to be taped and played back at the proper speed. He was given the codename Rowlands and a cryptic conversation to use when meeting contacts. They would say, 'I believe we met in Pittsburg in 1968', and Prime was to reply, 'No, at that time I was in Berlin.' He returned to London and the JTLS offices overlooking Blackfriars Bridge with a black attaché case. Concealed in its fake bottom were code pads, special carbon papers, pre-addressed envelopes to East Berlin and £400.

Prime's dedicated diligence delighted both his British bosses and his Moscow masters. Marriage to teacher Helena Organ in 1969 did not halt the flow of information to the KGB. Prime wrote nonsense letters to 'Laura' in East Berlin. Then, using the special carbon papers, he would pencil the real message invisibly between the lines. It showed up only under a fluoroscope. Sometimes he left information in dead-letter boxes for collection by contacts at the Soviet embassy, and picked up payments and congratulatory notes from other hiding places. They included a tree stump near Abbey Wood, a secret spot near Banstead railway station, Surrey, and a drop near a lake at Esher.

But late in 1972, as his marriage crumbled, Prime lost his code books and was no longer able to decipher instrucions. Though he wrote to East Berlin, explaining what had happened, the cagey KGB did nothing, perhaps fearing their man had been discovered. Lost and alone again as he and Helena headed for divorce, Prime became increasingly depressed and needed psychiatric treatment. But he kept his spying secret. And late in 1974, the Russians re-established contact. A man and a woman with heavy East European accents delivered another briefcase of espionage equipment, plus £400, to the home of his sister Gladys. Prime cheered up again. He was back in business.

In September 1975 he was summoned to the Austrian capital, Vienna, to meet his Soviet employers. Two agents in America had alerted them to Rhyolite satellites, sent up 35,405 km (22,000 miles) above Africa and Borneo to monitor the quantity and quality of long-range missiles installed in Eastern Europe. The American spies had passed on mechanical and electronic details, but Moscow needed to know how to understand the satellites' messages – and feed them false information. Prime had been cleared earlier that year for access to those secrets. And he took to Vienna a dossier of photographs which revealed them all. He returned to Britain £800 richer. The following May he was back in Austria, telling his contacts how well the false signals were deluding the West about Russia's rocket strength. It was a delusion that enabled Moscow to establish a commanding lead in the nuclear missile race, despite the 1972 Strategic Arms Limitation Treaty.

But the Rhyolite system was only part of Project Byeman, an ambitious series of satellites designed to allow the NATO powers unhindered observation of every aspect of Soviet life. It included Argus, a top secret space snooper which could eavesdrop on all microwave telecommunications in the USSR. Radio links between tank commanders on exercise, telephone talks between the Kremlin and missile site chiefs, even the Russian military computer system could be tapped or raided. Data was fed into computers like NSA's CRAY-1, capable of storing 30 billion words and making 150 million calculations per second. Codes could be instantly cracked, messages automatically translated, and strategically important messages sifted by a system of key-word recognition. But by the end of 1976, the KGB knew every detail of the surveillance thanks to Prime. For in March he had been transferred to one of the two nerve centres of the network, GCHQ in Cheltenham. And within months he was appointed analyst of decrypted intercepts in J Division, which handled every vital Soviet bloc communication monitored at ground stations in Europe, the Middle East and Cyprus. Prime was in charge of 30 staff who were ordered to show him all the most significant messages. And as a section head he sat in at planning meetings, which gave him access to information from other departments.

Prime could now tell the KGB exactly which codes and cyphers had been cracked, and pinpoint specific surveillance targets. By assessing areas of interest, Moscow could calculate areas of Western ignorance. And while adopting new codes for the real messages, it could feed false information by those known to be compromised. Fake facts fostered friction between the NATO partners, encouraged the West to waste time and resources developing the wrong weapons to counter non-existent Soviet build-ups, and manoeuvred defence forces in Western Europe into potentially disastrous positions. Experts were later to say that, had Russia invaded Germany during Prime's heyday, NATO would have been taken totally by surprise. And Prime, who had made the subterfuges possible, was still in a position to tell Moscow how well they were succeeding.

But by the middle of 1977, alarm bells were ringing in Washington. When transmissions controlling air traffic at Murmansk suddenly switched to a new wavelength, NSA warned GCHQ that there was almost certainly a Soviet spy inside Cheltenham. The Russians tipped off Prime, and he resigned in September rather than risk detection. Two months earlier he had married his landlady, Rhona Ratcliffe, and become stepfather to her three sons. They brought a £37,000 home, Laburnam Cottage in Pittville Crescent Lane, and Prime told inquirers that his new family life was the 'personal reason' for leaving his job at GCHQ. He added that the Cheltenham centre was 'too imperialistic, 50 years behind the times'. His lawyers were later to claim he could no longer live with the torment of being a double agent. The Russians, they said, had promised him a good pension if he defected to Moscow, and twice he booked flights to Helsinki, only to turn back as he neared Heathrow airport because he could not leave Rhona and the boys. In fact, there are good reasons for believing Prime was still an active Soviet agent.

He became a driver for the local Cheltex taxi company. Colleagues dubbed him Boris and Comrade Prime because he spent intervals between jobs sitting in his car reading Russian magazines or listening to Radio Moscow. Yet no one objected when he volunteered for regular runs to GCHQ, to drive staff home and collect or deliver documents and computer tapes. The job was perfect cover for his frequent visits to the spy centre, and enabled him to move round the region without arousing suspicion.

Spy scandals at Little Sai Wan, the Hong Kong listening post in Britain's worldwide surveillance network, were hushed up in 1961 and 1973. First a four man team headed by ex-policeman John Tsang was discovered sending daily reports to Peking, and deported. The Red Chinese recruited Tsang while he was studying at Cambridge University in England. Twelve years later, two Taiwanese radio operators defected behind the Bamboo Curtain, taking with them valuable information on their monitoring activities.

The KGB had certainly not lost interest in Prime. In May 1980 he flew to Vienna again and handed over 15 rolls of film containing 500 secret GCHQ documents during a three-day cruise on the Danube with his controllers. At his trial, it was said the films were taken during his final months on the GCHQ staff. Why the Russians were sufficiently impressed to pay £600 for them nearly three years later was never explained. In November 1981 Prime returned from Potsdam £4,000 richer, though he told the Old Bailey a year later that he could answer none of the KGB's queries about Cheltenham.

By then, Prime had fallen out with his taxi workmates and become a travelling salesman for a Bristol wine merchant. He was so bad at the job that he had to buy cases of bottles himself to keep his sales record up to scratch. But it was again excellent cover for clandestine movements. This time, though, the secrecy had nothing to do with espionage. Prime always suffered from sexual inadequacy. By 1980 he was compensating for it by forcing girls aged from 10 to 14 to expose themselves while he masturbated. Police interviewed him that April about an indecent assault in Cheltenham, but eliminated him from their inquiries. Instead of taking the warning to heart, he merely moved further afield. He meticulously built up a card index of 2,287 girls and their addresses from reports in local newspapers in Gloucestershire and Herefordshire. A pile of directories in his garage gave him their telephone numbers. The lucky ones merely received obscene calls. Others were cunningly chatted up to discover when they would be at home alone. Prime then called in person, posing as a handyman hired for painting or plumbing jobs.

For two years the ploy worked. But in April 1982, his luck ran out. He fled a house at Preston Wynne, Herefordshire, when his intended victim screamed. Neighbours had noted a distinctively coloured two-tone Cortina. Detectives painstakingly worked through a list of 426 registered owners of such cars. Six days after the attack, two police officers called at Laburnam

Cottage. Prime denied responsibility. But that night he told Rhona about both the sex attacks and his spying. Next morning, Friday 28 April, he telephoned police to admit three indecent assaults. He was taken into custody and charged. It was later surmised that, had he been arrested the previous evening, his espionage might never have been revealed. For he would not have been able to confess to his wife.

Rhona wrestled with her conscience for a further three weeks. Then she discovered a carrier bag under the marital bed. It contained what Sir Michael Havers was to call 'the indispensible tools of a modern spy,' a radio, tapes and black briefcase concealing notebooks and 26 envelopes with East Berlin addresses. After consulting her lawyer, doctor and parents, Rhona went to the police. Confronted with her statement, Prime at last agreed to discuss his treachery. And in the Old Bailey's No 1 court on 10 November 1982, he pleaded guilty to seven charges of passing information likely to be useful to an enemy between December 1967 and November 1981, plus three charges of indecent assault.

His devoted wife, who promised to stand by him, told the trial: 'He has changed. He has lost all his burden and is now a new man. He was a tortured personality.' Defending barrister George Carman pleaded eloquently for leniency, saying: 'It is the misfits of society that provide the fertile breeding ground for the ruthless propaganda of the Soviet system and its capacity to foster treachery under the guise of idealism.' But Lord Chief Justice Lane was unimpressed. 'I have been asked not to treat you as a ruthless and rationally motivated spy,' he told Prime. 'But I am bound to say that is a description which fits you perfectly.'

The traitor's 38 year sentence represented two consecutive 14 year terms for charges relating to his Vienna visits, deemed the most serious treachery, concurrent seven year imprisonment for the other five espionage charges, and three years for the indecent assaults. Prime Minister Margaret Thatcher made it clear through leaks to trusted journalists that Prime would never be exchanged for Westerners held behind the Iron Curtain. But she only admitted to the House of Commons that he had alerted the Russians to what

A spy ring inside British Army Intelligence passed information on Falklands battle plans to the Soviet embassy in London, senior officers revealed in November 1982. And it was feared by investigators that the secrets may later have been given to Argentine forces while they occupied the islands.

the West knew of their defences, and how the information was obtained. If she was furious over Prime the Americans were hopping mad. And for a while there were serious fears that pent-up anger which poured out from Pentagon and intelligence sources might sever the espionage links between the two countries. The Prime affair was described as the worst crisis of confidence since the Burgess-Maclean defections in 1951 and the worst blow to US intelligence for two decades. A Pentagon spokesman said: 'The Russians knew more about GCHQ than we did.' And there were dark hints that Prime was not working alone. He was 'just the tip of the iceberg', journalists in Washington were told. He knew the identity of at least three other moles at Cheltenham.

Britain's system of positive vetting for security clearance bore the brunt of the US attacks. Mrs Thatcher revealed that Prime had passed the test four times during his career. Positive vetting involves an employee filling in a questionnaire about interests and acquaintances, and giving the names of two people who can be approached for references. It is supposed to reveal peculiar sexual proclivities, wayward political opinions and personal problems brought about by drink, drugs or reckless spending. In fact, as Tory MP Sir Bernard Braine declared in Parliament, it has never unmasked the 'loners, perverts and drunkards' whose flaws are manipulated by the KGB. Dedicated agents can lie with impunity. Sir Timothy Kitson, chairman of the all-party Commons Committee on Defence, described positive vetting as a shambles. He was only echoing what Washington had believed for years. The NSA and CIA have constantly urged Britain's leaders to sacrifice respect for individual liberty in the interests of the tighter security ensured by polygraph lie detector tests, random telephone taps and surveillance, but in vain.

American anger at what they saw as British bungling and amateurism was heightened by their warnings of a mole in Cheltenham as early as 1977. And US fears were supported by Jock Kane, a GCHQ employee for nearly 30 years until 1978, who said he was certain another mole was still inside the organization, 'high up enough to influence reports which go to the Cabinet'. While the West had prior warning of the Soviet invasion of Czechoslovakia in 1968, it was taken by surprise by the 1979 incursion into Afghanistan and the 1980 crackdown on Poland. Kane claimed the flurry of intercepted diplomatic and military messages which must have preceded both events had either been 'lost', deliberately analysed wrongly, or cunningly concealed.

Staff still working at GCHQ were quick to tell the press of appalling security there. On the very day Prime was jailed, GCHQ placed advertisements in *The Times* for a Russian linguist, virtually inviting new moles to apply. A married couple claimed they took a Cheltenham desk computer home at weekends to play space games with their children. One man said plastic passes issued to all staff were hardly scrutinized. One day he had taken his wife's to work by mistake, and security men had not even noticed. A girl secretary alleged that one morning she arrived at the gates to find them open, and the guards asleep. Unvetted painters, decorators and maintenance men told of wandering round the buildings at night. And office workers revealed that lighters and other personal possessions had vanished from their desk drawers. They might just as easily have been top secret documents.

Both Britain and America had little choice but to bite their tongues, and try to salvage a relationship of trust from the debacle. The two nations knew that, whatever might be said in public, they needed each other's help in countering Soviet espionage and penetrating the Iron Curtain. President Reagan began a crash re-armament programme to counter the deficiencies Prime's treachery had created. NATO commanders re-appraised their battle plans. And the NSA sent a former deputy director, Benson K. Buffham, to review and strengthen security at Cheltenham.

For beyond the obvious questions – how did positive vetting fail to reveal both Prime's espionage and his criminal interest in under-age girls? How could he travel so freely to Iron Curtain countries without arousing suspicion, and walk through Customs carrying spy equipment? Did he compromise Western agents by enabling Moscow to trace leaks? Why did the KGB allow him to leave Cheltenham in 1977? – lay a deeper fear. When Prime's home was searched, police discovered literature from the Paedophile Information Exchange and an American organization that also catered for perverted sexual interests. They also found a comprehensive list assessing fellow workers at Cheltenham. Five were later demoted to jobs involving no access to secret papers on the strength of Prime's observations. And the frightening prospect was that Prime may have used his inside information and his links with strange sex cults to provide the KGB with material for blackmail traps.

Prime brought back to the public eye all the worries that had largely lain dormant since the flurry of spy scandals in the early 1960s. And they were heightened by the impact one man could have on costly space age secrets. Dr David Owen, once a Labour government foreign minister, but by 1982 a leader of the new Social Democrat Party in Britain, wrote in the *Daily Mail*:

'We are a little too smugly British about countering the would-be spy. In a filthy fight, we cannot really afford to continue playing to every nuance of the Queensberry rules. There is a war going on, and in wartime you have to adopt measures which are rougher and tougher than those you would normally contemplate ... We have got to catch these spies before they do the damage, not just lock them up when the secrets are out.'